Picking up the Pieces after Domestic Violence

of related interest

Rebuilding Lives after Domestic Violence
Understanding Long-Term Outcomes
Hilary Abrahams
ISBN 978 1 84310 961 7

Mothering Through Domestic Violence
Lorraine Radford and Marianne Hester
ISBN 978 1 84310 473 5

Talking About Domestic Abuse
A Photo Activity Workbook to Develop Communication
Between Mothers and Young People
Cathy Humphreys, Ravi K Thiara, Agnes Skamballis and Audrey Mullender
ISBN 978 1 84310 423 0

Talking To My Mum
A Picture Workbook for Workers, Mothers and
Children Affected by Domestic Abuse
Cathy Humphreys, Ravi K Thiara, Agnes Skamballis and Audrey Mullender
ISBN 978 1 84310 422 3

Supporting Women after Domestic Violence
Loss, Trauma and Recovery
Hilary Abrahams
Foreword by Cathy Humphreys
ISBN 978 1 84310 431 5

Making an Impact – Children and Domestic Violence
A Reader
2nd edition
Marianne Hester, Chris Pearson and Nicola Harwin
With Hilary Abrahams
ISBN 978 1 84310 157 4

Domestic Violence and Child Protection
Directions for Good Practice
Edited by Cathy Humphreys and Nicky Stanley
ISBN 978 1 84310 276 2

Counselling Survivors of Domestic Abuse
Christiane Sanderson
ISBN 978 1 84310 606 7

Picking up the Pieces after Domestic Violence

A Practical Resource for Supporting Parenting Skills

Kate Iwi and Chris Newman

Jessica Kingsley *Publishers*
London and Philadelphia

The Blob Tree on p.35 is from *Games Without Frontiers* by Pip Wilson © Pip Wilson and Ian Long and is reproduced with permission from Pip Wilson

First published in 2011
by Jessica Kingsley Publishers
116 Pentonville Road
London N1 9JB, UK
and
400 Market Street, Suite 400
Philadelphia, PA 19106, USA

www.jkp.com

Library of Congress Cataloging in Publication Data
Iwi, Kate, 1967-
  Picking up the pieces after domestic violence : a practical resource for supporting parenting skills / Kate Iwi and Chris Newman.
      p. cm.
  Includes bibliographical references.
  ISBN 978-1-84905-021-0 (alk. paper)
 1. Family violence. 2. Abused children--Psychology. 3. Parent and child.
4. Parenting. I. Newman, Chris, 1956- II. Title.

  HV6626.I95 2011
  362.82'924--dc22

                                   2010045775

British Library Cataloguing in Publication Data
A CIP catalogue record for this book is available from the British Library

ISBN 978 1 84905 021 0

Printed and bound in Great Britain

Contents

List of Figures

Worksheets

Handouts

1 Introduction

This book is aimed at workers who want to help parents to develop safe, protective and positive ways of caring for their children in the aftermath of a violent relationship. Each family will have its unique needs and so this book outlines a *risk and needs assessment* that will help you plan an intervention pathway on a case-by-case basis. The book is designed to be practical and full of exercises and techniques that might fit into that pathway. Some of the exercises we offer are very simple and require little specialist worker skill, whereas others are much more in-depth and complex. This book cannot take the place of the skills training, good clinical supervision and reflective practice, without which it will be difficult for most practitioners to simply 'read and try' a significant amount of the suggestions we offer. The writers of this book would simply caution practitioners to be selective – and to only try out techniques with clients where they feel able and clear about a given approach.

Designing an intervention pathway – and where this book fits in

- The first step will always be *managing immediate risks* and working to ensure the safety of all family members – this might involve making referrals to Children's Social Care, Multi-Agency Risk Assessment Conferences (MARACs), Independent Domestic Violence Advocates (IDVAs – for victim advocacy work), the charity Women's Aid (for refuge places) or local 'sanctuary schemes' (which can help make a safe sanctuary within the victim's own home). It is important to make links with the network of agencies working with domestic violence in your area – the local domestic violence forum (DVF) is a good place to start. If you have taken these steps but feel that some level of risk still remains, further resources are available in 'Safety planning' (see Chapter 3).

- The next step is *deciding what support the parents need to help them prioritise their own and their children's safety*. This might include:

  ◦ Support groups for victims. The Women's Aid national helpline 0800 2000 247 or your local DVF should be able to help you find support groups in your area.

  ◦ Domestic violence prevention programmes for abusers. Respect is the national membership organisation for domestic violence perpetrator programmes. Contact Respect on 020 7022 1801 to find out whether a programme is available locally.

- At the same time you might be looking for *specific services for the children* – your local Child and Adolescent Mental Health Services (CAMHS) can provide therapeutic services and a GP can refer to these even if they don't take self-referrals. Many areas also offer specialist groups for children and young people who've grown up with violence (contact your local DVF) or for those using violence themselves (contact Respect Young People's Services).

- You might also want to find less specific, *self esteem-building activities for the children* – resilience in children can be boosted by anything that increases their confidence and makes them less isolated, so as well as specific interventions, getting them involved in arts, drama or sports or finding them a mentor can be just as helpful. Get the school and local youth and family support services involved.

- Last but not least in the pathway is likely to be some direct work *healing and developing parenting skills* in the aftermath of the domestic violence – and that's where this book of resources comes in. You should begin by using the 'Parenting needs assessment' (see Chapter 2) to find out which of these resources parents or carers may need most – then just flip through to the resources and get started. We hope you'll find them helpful.

Parenting in the aftermath of domestic violence

A large body of research now shows that growing up with violence in the home can seriously affect children's development.[1] Of course, most parents who have suffered violence have worked hard to protect their children from the worst effects of it. For many, their parenting skills have remained intact and the ending of the violence may be enough to enable them to re-establish a positive environment for their children. However, most parents who have recently left or are leaving a violent relationship can really use some help facing the very difficult task of managing their own loss and recovery while also helping their children to heal. Furthermore, when their own personal resources may be at their lowest, they find they are required to step up to the task of parenting children who may not be securely attached, may be developmentally delayed, and may be 'acting out' in challenging ways rather than talking about their own feelings of hurt, fear, anger and loss.

Those who have perpetrated the violence also face a significant challenge if they wish to mend some of the damage they have caused. It was once thought that a man could abuse his partner but still somehow be a 'good father' to his children. However, this idea is no longer considered tenable; indeed, some research indicates that the fear and dread associated with threats to a child's main carer can have worse effects than direct assaults on the child – and the family courts in the UK have now recognised that domestic violence involves a 'very serious and significant failure in parenting'.[2] Even if the abusing parent leaves the home, he is rarely completely absent from the children's lives. He can be a powerful positive or negative influence on the well-being of the children. Most parents who've abused a partner can use some help to acknowledge the harm they've caused, and to learn how to parent the children in a way that helps them to recover a sense of safety and stability.

A note on gender

Violence in intimate relationships takes many forms, and can be inflicted by men on women, by women on men, within same-sex relationships, and may include collusion or direct abuse from other family members. Surveys that ask whether people have suffered *any* form of physical violence in intimate relationships tend to show that women are only slightly more likely to report suffering violence than men. However, when surveys ask about the *impact* of the violence, it tends to be women who report more severe violence, who are more likely to be injured and more likely to live their lives in fear of their partners. Even if women start out using violence in a relationship, men's greater physical strength often ends up shifting the power balance over time:

> I didn't call it domestic violence because I used to hit him too – I felt we were on even ground. But then it started to shift. Over time he became more aggressive. I would end up backing down and he wouldn't. Then I started to feel like I was getting bullied, I was avoiding saying things because I was scared of getting hurt.

This means that, when agencies are set up to work with perpetrators of domestic violence, it tends to be largely men who walk through the door. So in writing this book we draw on our experience of working with the thousands of men – and a few women – referred to our agencies because they have used violence in their intimate relationships. We strongly believe that all forms of abuse in intimate relationships are unacceptable and avoidable, whoever is the perpetrator. However, in this book we will often refer to those using abuse in relationships as men and victims as women – partly because this reflects our practice experience, but also because it avoids the awkwardness of expression that gender-neutral language creates. Most of the exercises and suggestions for working that we include here can be readily adapted whoever is the primary perpetrator of abuse in the relationship.

What is domestic violence?

It's important to start out with some kind of definition of what we mean when we talk about domestic violence. Any act of violence or abusive behaviour that takes place in an intimate or family relationship could be defined as domestic violence. However, most workers in the field feel it is important to somehow capture one of the key features that women who live with domestic violence report – that the victim ends up feeling *controlled* in their day-to-day lives by their partner. You don't need to experience violence very often before a threat, a warning look, or even a prolonged silence can act as a reminder of the violence and as a warning to get in line. This is why Women's Aid UK defines domestic violence (some people use the term 'domestic abuse') as a *pattern* of coercive and controlling behaviour that takes place within an intimate relationship. This can range from severe and repeated physical violence through to persistent emotional and psychological abuse, and financial control.

Above all, violence is a way of exerting power. In some cases this may be quite intentional on the part of the perpetrator, where he hits or threatens his partner as a way of establishing authority and setting the rules in the relationship. However, even where the conscious intention is less easy to identify, any violence or threatening behaviour has the effect of instilling fear in other members of the family and making them alter their own behaviour in an attempt to avoid further violence. This can range from 'treading on eggshells' to living in abject terror. What this means is that domestic violence systematically distorts the power relations in the family.

Domestic violence and family power dynamics

In any family, the adult carers have power over the children they care for, which, if things are working well, is used to protect and teach the children until they are able to function independently. Additionally, where things are working well, the adults should model power equality in respect of each other (the same principle applies whether these carers are biological parents or grandparents, step-parents or foster carers, a man and woman, a same-sex couple or an extended family group, whether they live together or whether they have equal responsibility for, or contact with, the children).

However, domestic violence distorts family systems. The abusive violent partner has more power than the other parent to set the rules in the family and to get his own way and to shut down dissent from other members of the family.

The abused parent in some cases may be barely above the children in the power relationship, and sometimes even below. This might be because the children have learned, or even been encouraged, to join in with the abuse. The abuser is, after all, the most important one in the family to please and to get on the right side of. More benignly, power relations in the family may shift if the children repeatedly witness the victimised parent in a state of injury or distress, and attempt to comfort and protect her. If the children feel they have to take on a protective role·towards their parent, the parent–child relationship has effectively been turned upside down. (Paradoxically, the abuser may end up looking like a more capable parent than the victim, whose abilities as a parent may have been severely damaged by the abuse).

Note: This book will not attempt to address issues of getting the adults safe from domestic violence – there are many others that deal with helping victims get safe or helping perpetrators stop their abuse. This book picks up where the domestic violence has ceased. This might be due to the abuser changing, but much more often it is because the couple have separated. (Please don't ever assume that separation marks the end of domestic violence – 54% of police call-outs for domestic violence occur in cases where the couple are no longer living together – see Chapter 2 on risk assessment and management).[3]

When the family separate, the impact is a bit like when you take off one part of a mobile – the sort we hang above our children's cots; the remainder swings wildly for a time and it's hard to predict how it will settle. Where there's been domestic violence, the family has been ruled by an iron fist. The abuser is likely to be physically abusive to the children also. (Research suggests that there is at least a 30% overlap between domestic violence and child abuse, and this climbs to around 60% for children in need of protection and to nearly 100% in more severe domestic violence cases).[4] Because it is most often the violent parent who has gone, the remaining parent just can't match that level of power. There's a power vacuum and what we all too often see is the children moving up to take over. With older teenagers that can mean their ruling the roost and using violence and abuse towards their single remaining parent. Even children as young as two or three can appear to have taken over – with the parent appearing to be absolutely wrapped around the finger of a powerful infant, unable to hold boundaries at all in the face of fierce tantrums.

A continuum of parenting styles

Figure 1.1 below shows the continuum of parenting styles that may be present where violence and abuse have played a significant part in the life of the family. This continuum provides a framework for the interventions set out in this book.

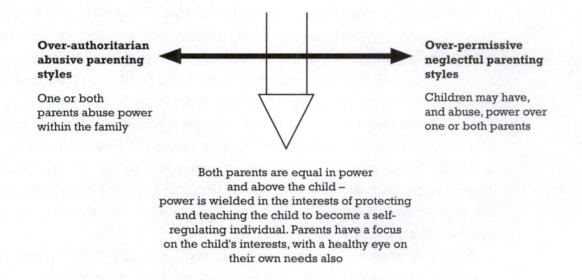

Over-authoritarian abusive parenting styles

One or both parents abuse power within the family

Over-permissive neglectful parenting styles

Children may have, and abuse, power over one or both parents

Both parents are equal in power and above the child – power is wielded in the interests of protecting and teaching the child to become a self-regulating individual. Parents have a focus on the child's interests, with a healthy eye on their own needs also

Figure 1.1 'Good enough' parenting

Often following domestic violence we are dealing with an abusive parent who is at the over-authoritarian, abusive end of the parenting continuum, and an abused parent who is at the over-permissive, neglectful end of the parenting continuum. However, this is not always the case and that's why the whole premise of this book is that where parenting interventions are concerned, ONE SIZE DOES NOT FIT ALL. Experience tells us that a substantial minority of domestic violence perpetrators tend more towards an over-permissive, neglectful style of parenting just as there is a substantial minority of domestic violence victims or survivors who both have and considerably abuse power over their children. This is why the book offers a needs assessment section and isn't simply divided into 'interventions for victims as parents' and 'interventions for abusers as parents'.

Helping parents towards the zone of 'good enough' parenting

What this book sets out to do is to provide some tools and techniques to help to move parents back into the zone of 'good enough' parenting (see Figure 1.2). It's somewhat of a relief to remember that there *can be no perfect parent* – that all parents get it wrong sometimes and in some ways. Indeed we will be suggesting that getting things a bit wrong and repairing them is one of the vital functions of good enough parenting, developing in the child a vital faith in the possibility of healing and mending as well as modelling the skills needed for this.

While most 'universal' parenting programmes' work on refining parenting that's already within, or very close to, the 'good enough' zone, there are also a few programmes and interventions designed specifically to bring parents from the more extreme ends of the parenting continuum towards good enough parenting, and for this book we have drawn heavily on the ones of these we think are most specifically useful in the wake of domestic violence. For example, we have taken some materials from 'Caring Dads', developed in Ontario for abusive fathers – which we think are particularly appropriate for parents with an overblown sense of entitlement over their children and with abusively authoritarian parenting styles. We have also picked out some parts of 'Who's in Charge?' – a programme from Melbourne, Australia, for parents of 'out-of-control' children – which we found particularly appropriate for parents who need to get more assertive with their children.

Once parents have a clearer idea about the circumstances in which it is acceptable to discipline a child – for authoritarian parents that would mean cutting back on discipline and thinking more about their children's rights, but for over-permissive parents it would mean stepping up the discipline and thinking more about their own rights – all parents can make use of the kinds of non-abusive behaviour management techniques that most 'standard' parenting programmes offer.

Of course, some of our parents may struggle to learn from any of this material without some work on issues from their own childhoods that block them from doing so. We cover this in 'Parents' own childhoods' Chapter 5. This kind of work may be a prerequisite to bringing some parents into the zone of 'good enough' parenting.

On the other hand, the children themselves will have been affected by the domestic violence and some of them will already be showing significant signs of the resulting harm. The more traumatised and less resilient the children are, the more their parents may be required to step up their parenting to deal with their sometimes bizarre, sometimes frightening and sometimes terrified acting out.

Parents will need a more therapeutic style of parenting to manage this kind of behaviour effectively and this will also be covered towards the end of the book.

Note: There's an important safety warning here. It will be almost impossible to work on positive parenting if the physical safety of the parents and children is not assured. It is premature to work on child-centred parenting if one of the parents is still using violence or threats of violence.

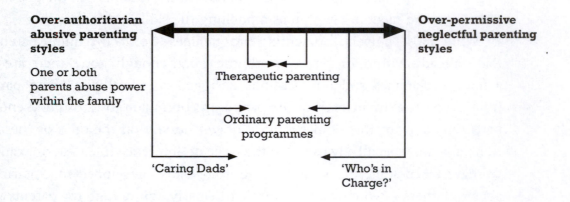

Figure 1.2 Zone of 'good enough' parenting

2 Assessing and Managing Risk

In this chapter and Chapter 3 we've laid out a framework on the following.

1. A session with parent/s alone to assess risk and needs.

2. A session to help you and the family gain a richer sense of the family's strengths and resources. This session is ideally done as a family, but can be with a child or parent alone.

3. Setting goals for your work together.

4. Safety planning for cases where there is current risk.

This book is designed for working with parents after the abuse has stopped. However, while the information from the parents, or from the agency that referred them to you, may indicate that the violence or abuse is in the past, it is important to explore the parents' current situation and to continue to monitor for signs of the violence restarting. There's a hierarchy of need here – it will be almost impossible to work on positive parenting if the physical safety of the parents and children is not assured.

This is particularly the case because the abusing parent is likely to be present in the children's lives regardless of whether or not the couple continue to live together. (The number of cases where contact is permanently denied by the courts in the UK is very small – fewer than 1%).

It is common for the abusing parent to continue to use violence, abuse and controlling behaviour long after the parents have separated. Even if the physical violence has stopped, the non-abusing parent may still be experiencing harassment or threats – and the fear of further violence may have led to her agreeing to unsatisfactory and unsafe contact arrangements. Even where things look pretty calm, the abuse often suddenly starts again if circumstances change – for instance, if the mother starts a new relationship after separation.

Parents who are still living together may be unwilling or embarrassed to disclose that they are still experiencing abuse, particularly if they are afraid of children's services intervention. Still others may be experiencing persistent abuse, but may not have defined their experiences as being 'domestic violence'.

Even if the domestic violence has stopped, either parent may continue to pose a risk to the child – through neglectful or abusive parenting, undermining the non-abusing parent, or through exposing the child to violence and abuse in a new relationship.

Finally, to complicate things still further, older children may well have learned enough from the domestic violence they've lived through to start being dangerously abusive themselves to siblings or parents.

Above all, our primary responsibility is to ensure the safety of the parents and children we are working with, and we cannot do this if we do not work with an ongoing awareness of the potential for harm.

As a result, before you start to work with a parent, it is important to determine the following.

- What is the current level of risk to that parent?

- What is the current risk of physical or emotional harm to the child? (The answer to these questions might not be the same – for instance, if the parents have separated, but the child is visiting the violent parent for contact visits at weekends).

- If you are working with the parent who has been abusive, what risk does he pose to his partner and children?

The answers to these questions will help you decide how to work with the parent – whether your work needs to be primarily safety-focused, or focused on recovery and positive parenting.

Risk assessment

Risk assessment is a complex area, and we do not propose to cover it in detail here. However, there are some key things to remember.

Risk assessment is an ongoing process – while you might use a structured assessment format or risk assessment tool at the start of your work, it is equally important to continue to be vigilant for changes in presentation, behaviour or circumstance that should set alarm bells ringing about safety.

Cooperation with other agencies – it is important to work in collaboration with other agencies to ensure that working with the abusive parent does not increase risk to the non-abusing parent and children. This is especially the case if you feel that the abusive parent's participation in the work you are doing may be taken as evidence of reduction in risk, and to persuade the partner, the courts or other agencies to relax restrictions that have been put in place to safeguard the children.

Risk assessment relies on good information – both your own and that of other agencies. Neither you nor any other single agency are likely to have a full picture of the family's situation. That means that ongoing information sharing is vital – a bit of information you hold may form an important part of the overall jigsaw.

You should always refer a child to the local authority Children's Social Care, if you believe that the child either is suffering, or is likely to suffer, significant harm.

Similarly, although the thresholds are higher, you should refer an adult at risk of serious harm to your local MARAC.

Safe working practices

We do not want our working practices to add to risk. This means that we need some basic safety principles. You should avoid disclosing things that other family members have said in front of someone who might have a dangerous response. This means you need to be clear in your own mind, and with other professionals, as to who has told you what. It may also require your insisting that parts of case conferences or similar meetings take place with risky family members excluded. However, if disclosure of any information you hold would decrease the likely risk of significant harm to a child or the serious risk of harm to an adult, then you must disclose. Explain to all the family members the principles you will follow regarding the use and disclosure of confidential information.

Plan very carefully for interviews

We suggest that you begin your work assessing the risks in the family which means *seeing each family member separately*. If you start off with a family group for whatever reason then start doing the work on strength building first (see Chapter 3). Then go on to arrange separate meetings with individual family members to look into the problems and risks as they see them.

Risk areas or factors

Once you have a chance to talk to the family members separately, it is best to have prepared a list of key areas to ask about, or a risk factor checklist, just to make sure you don't miss key information. The best indicator of risk is the history of violence and abuse, which is why it is good practice in risk assessment to seek information from case files as well as interviewing. Additionally, if we ask parents a general question such as 'Are you experiencing domestic violence?', we are quite likely to get a negative response. Both perpetrators and victims may have quite restrictive definitions of violence so it can be very helpful to use checklists, or a list of questions, about specific abusive behaviours.

At the end of this chapter we have included a risk assessment tool, developed by Co-ordinated Action Against Domestic Abuse (CAADA) and the Association of Chief Police Officers (ACPO), which you can use to ensure you cover the main bases. A lot of these tools are available in the field – whichever tool you use, it is important to be aware of what kind of risk it was designed to assess, and to whom – the CAADA-DASH tool, for instance, is used by the police and other agencies in assessing the current risk of serious harm to adult victims of domestic violence.

Besides information on perpetrators' history of physical or sexual abuse and neglect of their children, and the level of continued danger to the non-abusing parents, you will also need to know about:

- both parents' history of neglect or abuse of the children
- the history of the children being used in or exposed to violent events
- the level of coercive control that the predominant perpetrator has exercised in the past
- the history of handling contact arrangements
- the history of substance abuse and mental illness in the family generally
- the history of abuse by older children of either parents or younger siblings
- the history of abuse by extended family members
- the level of willingness of those who pose risks to other family members to accept the decisions of the victim and of social institutions such as law enforcement and the courts
- the risk of child abduction.

How do I know if it's safe enough to work with parents together?

You may be asked to work with a family where there has been domestic violence in the past and the parents are still living together. How can we judge whether parenting work, which directly addresses the topic of domestic violence, is safe to do with both parents together? For a start you will need to begin working with them separately in order to assess this. Never assume that just because a couple live together you can't make their situation more risky by working with them together. Run your usual assessment, or use something like the interview suggested later in this chapter, and ask yourself the following questions to help you decide.

- How long is it since the last violence? Workers need to consider the previous pattern of violence. If this has involved very frequent low-level violence, then one year's cessation of violence indicates a substantial change in pattern and an acceptably low risk of re-assault to consider parenting work. On the other hand, in a case of intermittent and serious violence, then a period of one year violence-free may not necessarily indicate any change in the risk and pattern of violence and a considerably longer period of monitoring will be needed

- Does she think he will be violent again?

- Does she feel safe to express herself, both during and outside sessions – is she likely to suffer consequences if she speaks out of turn?

- Does she believe that she is now safe to disagree with her partner, especially around parenting issues, to confront difficult topics and to express anger towards him, and that she can do so without fear of violence or abuse?

- Does she blame herself or does she recognise his responsibility for his behaviour?

- Does the parent who was violent feel ready to face up to the effects of his behaviour on his partner and children, and to talk about this without being angry or abusive in sessions?

If things change or one of the parents gets abusive in a session, then return them to separate sessions immediately.

Risk to workers

Lastly, it is important to remember that working with domestic violence can expose workers to physical risk, and we need to be demanding about our own safety. We owe it to ourselves, to our service users for whom we should model self-care, and to our children and significant others. The following points may help in setting up safe working practices.

- Ensure that you carry out risk interviews in a safe working environment with other adults around.

- Do not do challenging and exploratory work on home visits. Home visits are ideal for observation or for strength-building work but not for detailed interviews.

- Read chronologies and reports, before seeing service users, for indications of risk to professionals.

- In cases where you are concerned about the risk to workers, discuss this with your line manager.

- Fear is a very important indicator – don't be ashamed to come forward about it.

Safeguards might include:

- choice of venue

- having a second person present

- explaining that you will be asking difficult direct questions and that you want to do so safely

- explaining that it isn't OK to shout, damage objects, or threaten or hurt you

- asking the service user how they can reassure you that they will not behave in such ways, even if they feel really frustrated with your questions

- agreeing to have a time-out part-way through an interview if needed

- warning a fellow worker and having them on hand within earshot

- checking whether your agency has a well-known and practised plan, in your local office, for what should happen if a worker sounds the panic alarm

- positioning your self in relation to doors and panic buttons

- checking objects in the room and removing those that lend themselves easily as weapons.

You should also monitor the state of the interviewee and your own anxiety or fear levels. If you are getting worried about either of these, then you might try:

- explaining that these are 'standard' questions, which you ask of everybody

- acknowledging frustrations and discomforts

- changing the direction of your questioning

- suggesting a break or drawing the interview to a close.

The next few pages offer some example interview questions that you might find helpful.

Assessment interview with a domestic violence victim

The following are a series of suggestions as to the kinds of questions you may want to ask in the course of the first few sessions with a client when you are wanting to gather a lot of information quickly in order to assess risk and plan your intervention pathway. This is not a script. If you simply ran through this many questions, it's unlikely your client will come a second time – and at any rate, many of the suggestions below are different ways of asking the same things. We suggest you read through and adapt some of them into your own natural way of talking to add into your usual assessment style and schedule.

Getting started

- In order to assess what help you may need, I'd like to ask you some very direct questions about your relationship – is that OK?

- I realise you don't know me from Adam and I'm going to ask you some very personal questions, so, if I overstep the mark for you, would you let me know somehow please?

- When did you meet? When did the relationship start getting serious? How soon did you move in together or marry?

- What did you see in your partner when you first met? How did he make you feel at first?

History of domestic violence

- What issues did you argue over at first? And later?

- When did you first get even slightly worried about the way he dealt with his anger?

- What were the earliest signs he might be a bit of bully?

- What is he like when he is angry – at his best and worst?

- When did he first lay a hand on you in anger?

- How does he get physical with you when arguing? If you could see a film of him during an argument, how would it look? Does he pace around, shout, bang things, break things, stand close to you when he is shouting?

- How long do arguments last? How do they end?

- How often do arguments like this happen?

- I use a wider definition of violence than some people – if you think of pushing you, or holding you by the shoulders, or breaking things in the house as violence, how often did he do this kind of stuff?

- What is most frightening about him and his behaviour?

- What bothers you most about all this? What do you feel is the worst thing he's done to you?

I know this is difficult to talk about – this is not about making you feel bad, this is just about increasing your safety, which means being able to assess the risk. I need to try to form a clear picture for myself so we know what we're dealing with. When the worst incident took place…

- Where was he? Where were you? Where were the children? What was happening before it started? What violence was used? How much force? To where on the body? Did you fall or hit against something? With what impact on you? Were you hurt? How many times did he hit you? etc. It is useful to use scales – on a scale of 1–5 (5 being punching you as hard as possible) how hard did he punch you?

- Have the police been called in the past? How many times?

Vulnerability-related issues

I'm going to ask you some questions about other issues in order to assess what your support needs might be – I am not thinking that any of these things mean you are even slightly to blame for being abused…

- Do you have any problems with alcohol or drugs (past or recent)? How much do you use per week?

- Do you have any health or mental health problems?

- Have you been hurt sexually or physically in your own past or childhood – you don't have to tell me details here of what happened if you don't want to.

- Have you ever felt like killing or hurting yourself? Have you made threats of or attempted suicide?

- Have you had any major life stresses lately – like bereavement or unemployment?

- Are you still with your partner? Are you considering splitting up?

- Are there child contact disputes?

Parenting issues

Tell me a bit about each of your children.

- What makes you proud of them?

- What things do they struggle with more than other kids their age?

- How did you hope being a parent would be? What's working? What are the best times for you as a parent?

- What are the hardest times for you?

- How has the violence in your relationship affected your relationship with your children?

- What do you think they are aware of?

- What have you noticed about how the children are affected by the violence and abuse between you and your partner?

- Did they see the violence? (If she says they were not in same room, ask where they were in the house).

- What do you think the effect of growing up seeing dad hit/insult/shout at mum can be on children?

- Do you talk with your children about the violence and conflict in the family? What do you say? What would you want to say, if you could?

- Is there anyone else the children talk to about this? Who else is important to them?

- What do you find hardest about each child's behaviour? Tell me about a time when your children have misbehaved. Why do you think they act like that?

- How do you try to manage that, at your best and when you're at your worst? What kinds of discipline do you use? What happens if this doesn't work? Do the kids sometimes get smacked?

- Do you and the children's father agree about how to discipline them?

- Have any of the children ever hurt or frightened you?

Her childhood

- What were things like between your parents or carers?

- What was it like when they argued and fought?

- Did you see or hear violence between them when you were a child?

- Did you ever get hurt yourself?

- Some people talk about being neglected or treated roughly as a child. Did anything like this happen to you?

- Who do you think was to blame for their violence?

- Did they ever get help?

Returning to own relationship and getting help

- Who do you think is to blame for the violence in your own relationship?

- What would have to change in order for you to feel safe? Safe to get angry and to express yourself without fear of reprisals?

- What do you think (be as realistic as possible) it would take for you to decide to leave? Would that be too late?

- Has he ever said he'll change or won't do it again? Did he keep his word?

- Have you ever thought about leaving? How did he or you change your mind?

- So you've been together X years and he's gone from (first bullying behaviour) to (worst bullying behaviour). If the violence and abuse continued to escalate in the same manner, where would your relationship be another X years down the line?

- You said that when you were first together he made you feel… How has his violence made you feel?

Assessment interview with a domestic violence perpetrator

Getting started

- In order to assess what help you may need, I'd like to ask you some very direct questions about your relationship and what you've done – is that OK?

- If I overstep the mark for you, will you let me know?

- When did you meet? When did the relationship start getting serious? How soon did you move in together or marry?

- What did you see in your partner when you first met? What did she see in you, do you think? How did you make her feel at first?

History of domestic violence

- What issues did you argue over at first? And later?

- When did you first get worried about how you deal with anger?

- When did you first lay a hand on your partner in anger?

- Tell me about some other times when you've gone too far? Or when you haven't used the right methods to stand up for yourself?

- What are you like these days when you are angry? At your best and at your worst?

- How do you get physical with your partner when arguing? If you could see a film of yourself during an argument, how would you look? Do you pace around, shout, bang things, break things, stand close to her when you are shouting?

- How long do arguments last? How do they end?

- How often do arguments like this happen?

- What do you feel is the worst thing you've done to your partner? What would your partner say is the worst thing?

- What is the most recent thing you've done?

- Have you ever got her to do sexual things that retrospectively you think she was uncomfortable about? How did you get her to do that?

- Tell me about your earlier relationships and in what ways they were similar and different from this.

- Have the police been called in the past? How many times?

- Any social services' involvement?

Risk-related issues

- Do you have any problems with alcohol or drugs (past or recent)?

- How much do you use per week?

- Is your drug or alcohol use related to use of violence?

- Will drug or alcohol use get in the way of participation in the programme? (Will you be able to refrain from use for 24 hours before the session?) If not, you may have to think about referral to a drug or alcohol agency.

- Do you have any mental health problems?

- Have you ever felt like killing or hurting yourself? Have you made threats of or attempted suicide?

- Have you had any major life stresses lately – like bereavement or unemployment?

- Are you still with your partner? Are you afraid you may split up?

- Are there child contact disputes?

Parenting issues

- Tell me a bit about each of your children.

- What makes you proud of them?

- What things do they struggle with more than other kids their age?

- How did you hope being a parent would be?

- What's working?

- What are the best times for you as a parent?

- What are the hardest times for you?

- How has the violence in your relationship affected your relationship with your children?

- What do you think they are aware of?

- What have you noticed about how the children are affected by the violence and abuse between you and your partner?

- Do you talk with your children about the violence and conflict in the family? What do you say? What would you want to say, if you could?

- Is there anyone else the children talk to about this? Who else is important to them?

- What do you find hardest about each child's behaviour? Tell me about a time when your children have misbehaved. Why do you think they act like that?

- How do you try to manage that, at your best and when you're at your worst? What kinds of discipline do you use? What happens if this doesn't work? Do the kids sometimes get smacked? Do you and the children's mother agree about how to discipline them?

- Did they see the violence? (If he says they were not in same room, ask where they were in the house).

- How do you think seeing the violence affected the kids? If they weren't in the room, how would they have felt listening to what went on? Or seeing the after-effects? (Ask if there was damaged property, injuries to their mother. Would the children have seen this?)

- What do you think the effect of growing up seeing dad hit/insult/shout at mum is on the children?

His childhood

- What were things like between your parents or carers?

- What was it like when they argued and fought?

- Did you see or hear violence between them when you were a child?

- Did you ever get hurt yourself?

- Some people talk about being neglected or treated roughly as a child. Did anything like this happen to you?

- Who do you think was to blame for the violence?

- Did they ever get help?

Returning to own relationship and taking action

- Who do you think is to blame for the violence in your own relationship?

- So you've been together X years and you've gone from (first bullying behaviour) to (worst bullying behaviour). If the violence and abuse continued to escalate in the same manner, where would your relationship be another X years down the line?

- You said that when you were first together you made her feel... How has your violence made her feel?

- How do you want to be as a partner and father? Is it different from how you've been? In what way?

- How do you feel about coming in for (X sessions) like this? Do you feel able to commit to this?

- Have you tried doing a course before (on any subject)? If you didn't finish it or go regularly why was that?

- Have you ever said you'll change or won't do it again? Did you keep your word? What got in the way?

CAADA-DASH MARAC Risk Indicator Checklist

For the identification of high-risk cases of domestic abuse, stalking and 'honour'-based violence. (For reference only: detailed guidance on how to use this assessment is available from www.caada.org.uk)

1. Has the current incident resulted in injury? (Please state what and whether this is the first injury.)

2. Are you very frightened?

3. What are you afraid of? Is it further injury or violence? (Please give an indication of what you think (name of abuser[s]) might do and to whom, including children.)

4. Do you feel isolated from family/friends – that is, does (......................) try to stop you from seeing friends/family/doctor or others?

5. Are you feeling depressed or having suicidal thoughts?

6. Have you separated or tried to separate from (......................) within the past year?

7. Is there conflict over child contact?

8. Does (......................) constantly text, call, contact, follow, stalk or harass you? (Please expand to identify what and whether you believe that this is done deliberately to intimidate you. Consider the context and behaviour of what is being done.)

9. Are you pregnant or have you recently had a baby (within the last 18 months)?

10. Is the abuse happening more often?

11. Is the abuse getting worse?

12. Does (......................) try to control everything you do and/or are they excessively jealous? (In terms of relationships, who you see, being 'policed at home', telling you what to wear for example. Consider 'honour'-based violence and specify behaviour.)

13. Has (......................) ever used weapons or objects to hurt you?

14. Has (......................) ever threatened to kill you or someone else and you believed them? (If yes, tick whom.)

    ☐ You

    ☐ Children

    ☐ Other (please specify)

15. Has (......................) ever attempted to strangle/choke/suffocate/drown you?

16. Does (.....................) do or say things of a sexual nature that make you feel bad or that physically hurt you or someone else? (If someone else, specify whom.)

17. Is there any other person who has threatened you or who you are afraid of? (If yes, please specify whom and why. Consider extended family if honour-based violence.)

18. Do you know if (.....................) has hurt anyone else? (Please specify whom including the children, siblings or elderly relatives. Consider honour-based violence.)

19. Has (.....................) ever mistreated an animal or the family pet?

20. Are there any financial issues? For example, are you dependent on (.....................) for money/have they recently lost their job/other financial issues?

21. Has (.....................) had problems in the past year with drugs (prescription or other), alcohol or mental health leading to problems in leading a normal life? (If yes, please specify which and give relevant details if known.)

22. Has (.....................) ever threatened or attempted suicide?

23. Has (.....................) ever broken bail/an injunction and/or formal agreement for when they can see you and/or the children? (You may wish to consider this in relation to an ex-partner of the perpetrator if relevant.)

24. Do you know if (.....................) has ever been in trouble with the police or has a criminal history? (If yes, please specify whether

    ☐ Domestic violence

    ☐ Sexual violence

    ☐ Other violence

    ☐ Other (please specify)

For consideration by professional: Is there any other relevant information (from victim or professional) that may increase risk levels? Consider victim's situation in relation to disability, substance misuse, mental health issues, cultural/language barriers, 'honour'-based systems and minimisation. Are they willing to engage with your service? Describe:

Parenting needs assessment

It is possible to get an idea of parenting needs by asking the relatively few questions in the suggested interview schedule. Using the table below, start to build a plan of work by matching the findings from your parenting needs assessment with materials in this book that are appropriate to the parenting needs you have identified.

Assessment finding	Relevant tools or sections	page
There is violence or abuse between adult family members (or severe violence from child to parent)	Risk assessment. Where the likelihood of harm is high, change the focus of work to safety planning and consider referral to child protection and specialist domestic violence agencies. Where risk of immediate harm is within your agency's working guidelines: Safety planning	17 43
Parent doesn't know the child/ren well and/or is focused on the negatives about their child/ren	Positive regard for my child Drawing out richer descriptions of family strengths	37 36
Parent lacks techniques for consistent non-abusive discipline	What counts as abuse? Steps for child-centred behaviour management	46 54
Parent is in denial/lacks empathy with the children's needs and the effects of parental domestic violence on them	Icebergs – exercise Building child empathy Child empathy role play – exercise	61 69 71
Parent lacks knowledge about how domestic violence can affect children	Educational materials on the effects of domestic violence	62
Parent is not able to talk about the violence and abuse in ways that support the children	Talking to children about violence and abuse	74
Issues from the parents' own childhood are affecting their parenting	Parents' own childhoods Own parents – exercise and discussion questions	77 79
Parent has unrealistic expectations of the children's developmental abilities	Educational handouts on developmental stages, 0–2, 2–4, 5–6, 7–11, 12–16, 17–19	82
Children in the family have control of parents and are abusive or violent to them in age-inappropriate ways	What counts as abuse? Child to parent violence and out-of-control behaviour Is it all my fault? – exercise Exploring guilt and shame – exercise Why does my teenager abuse me? – exercise Putting clear boundaries in place	46 97 101 104 105 107

Assessment finding	Relevant tools or section	page
Parent is too parent-centred and authoritarian	The parenting log – exercise and handout	115
	Undermining shame and fear-based methods of discipline	49
	The idea of child-centred parenting – exercise	50
	Explaining the impacts of domestic violence on children	62
Parent is angry at partner, the family courts or social services leading to abusive or self-destructive behaviour	The wall – exercise	44
	Tips for fathers – handout	128
	Tips for mothers – handout	133
Child appears to be traumatised and 'acting out'; parent has fair parenting capacity (stability and capacity to understand)	The effects of domestic violence on infants (attachment styles)	63
	Understanding and responding to a child who is 'acting out' – handout	121
	Empathetic parenting with children who are 'acting out'	118
The parent–child bond is weak	Talking to children about violence and abuse	74
	Drawing out richer descriptions of family strengths	37
	Positive regard for my child	36
Issues of guilt and self-blame	Exploring guilt and shame – exercise	104
	Is it all my fault? – exercise	101
Child is isolated from support networks	Utilising wider family and social networks – exercise	113
Parent has been abused in own intimate relationship	The effects of secrecy – exercise and discussion	74
	Tips for mothers – handout	133
Parent has used abuse in own intimate relationship	Tips for fathers – handout	128
Parent has been violent in the past Parent is using physical punishment or fear-based discipline with the children	Discipline	49
	Undermining shame and fear-based methods of discipline	49
	Impacts of shaming and put-downs – exercise	50
	The idea of child-centred parenting – exercise	50
	Problems with physical punishment of children – handout	52

3 Starting Out – Building Strengths, Setting Goals and Planning for Safety

Drawing out richer descriptions of family strengths

Where you have a chance to do work with the family, starting out with a strength-based approach can do wonders. By the time parents and children come forward for family sessions, the family's sense of their own strengths and the love they have for each other may have dwindled to dying embers. This work (based on the work of David Epston [2009])[6] is aimed at fanning the embers back to life – helping the family build richer descriptions of the positive elements of the family relationships and of the strengths the family already have to tackle the problem. Below is a series of the kinds of questions and statements that will help. (Don't try to use them like a script – they are more of a guide for a conversation, which you can adapt according to whether you are working with one or more members of the family).

Identifying the child's strengths

- I know you and your family have got a problem or two but is it OK if we don't talk about that today? Instead I want to find out what strengths and qualities you have first.

- Can you tell me about your strengths, what you're good at?

- If we were shipwrecked on a desert island, what would I come to appreciate about you? What would I come to depend on you for?

- What do you call this ability to do…?

- Can you tell me about a time when you did that? How did you decide to do that? Can you remember having that thought? What led up to it? What was it like? What were you doing? Where were you?

Helping the parent to identify the child's strengths

- If these questions are a bit hard, can I ask your mum so that I can see you through her eyes?

- [to mum] What makes you proud as a mother? If you were going to brag about…, what would you say?

- What should I know and appreciate about…(you know her well)?

- Can you give me an example of that? Could you tell me a story about this that would really illustrate what you meant by…?

- What is it about her that reassures you you're a good mother?

- What has she got that's wonderful about her that will help her tackle this problem? What are some other good things about her that other people comment on? What do her friends like best about her?

Legacy – helping the family to identify the parents' strengths

- [to child] Where do you get that quality from?

- Did you get that a bit from your mum?

- What's the best lesson in…she's taught you?

- [to mum] Did you hope [your daughter] would have this quality? Tell me a story to illustrate how you encouraged this quality? What would your own mother say if I was to ask her, 'When you see your granddaughter, do you see a bit of your daughter in her? Would she feel proud of that?'

Reverse legacy – identifying the positive influence of the child on the parent

- [to child] Do you think you were an inspiration for your mum? What have you done that could have been an inspiration for her?

- What could she have seen about you that might have inspired her?

- If your mum was looking down over your life from on high, what could she have learned about…?

- [to mum] Has [your daughter] been an inspiration to you? How?

- Has being her mother led you to live your life differently? Has she taught you anything about how to live life?

Working together

- Does your…and your mum's qualities always march side by side or do they sometimes run up against each other?

- If they marched side by side, where would you be able to get to? You would be pretty unstoppable…

You might want to set homework on this such as the following exercise.

✎ Exercise – Positive regard for my child
Aims

- To build the parent's ability to give praise.

- To help the parent begin to reflect on the child's needs.

- To help you assess the parent's ability to do so.

The 'Positive regard for my child' worksheet is designed to be given as a homework task in the early stages of your work with the parent and discussed during sessions – there should be one for each child.

The Blob Tree is an engaging visual aid to look at how each family member is approaching their work with you – it is always helpful to acknowledge the hopes and fears people come in with. Let everyone pick which Blob person they identify with right now and why.

Figure 3.1 The Blob Tree
Copyright © Pip Wilson from Games with Frontiers ISBN: 0551015543 published by
Marshall Pickering imprint of Harper Collins Publishing. Not to be published without
permission from pip@pipwilson.com, www.blobtree.com.

Positive regard for my child

Fill out one worksheet for each child.

Name of child . . . .   Age of child . . . .

The following are some of the qualities I love about my child:

. . . .

. . . .

. . . .

. . . .

The following are some of the things my child is good at:

. . . .

. . . .

. . . .

. . . .

The following are some of the qualities or talents I think my child is proud of:

. . . .

. . . .

. . . .

. . . .

✔

The following are some of the ways I am a good parent/some of the things I think my child loves about me:

....

....

....

....

I think my child feels angry or upset with me because of the following:

....

....

....

....

The following are some of the ways I think my child wants support from me:

....

....

....

....

If I kept in mind these things, I would behave differently as follows:

....

....

....

....

Introducing the problem

- By the way, what is the problem from your point of view?

Cutting the problem down to size

- So do you think the fact that you and your family are…(listing strengths)…might intimidate and shrink this 'problem' down to size? If you harnessed all these strengths, do you think you might really tackle those problems?

Starting with the child's answer, you can then find out more from the parents and move onto a discussion of family goals. At this stage it is useful to have a structure for the discussion – agree speaking time and don't let this part of the session deteriorate into an argument. If you have a small family group, you may want to ask another member of the family to comment on what they have heard, but otherwise discourage lengthy discussions.

Setting goals for your work together

If the work you do together is to have lasting value, it will be because the parents are engaged in working towards their own goals for their parenting. So it is useful to start with a discussion of what kind of relationship they want with their children, what their hopes are for their children, what kind of parents they want to be and why.

If you are working with both parents together, there may be some disagreement on the 'how' of parenting; however, there is less likely to be disagreement on the parents' long-term goals for their children (nearly all parents want their children to feel loved, to grow up and be happy, responsible, loving, etc.). So try to find ways of framing each parent's goals in a way that fits with their shared long-term goals. With children and young people, goal setting can be restricted to a discussion of how they want their family life to be and what they think is getting in the way of that. A teenage girl may not want to sign up to a goal that states that she should come in earlier and do her homework on time, but she is likely to want to get on better with her mum and dad, or, failing this, at least to get them off her back.

✐ Exercise – Setting goals with parents

Ask the parents to choose and label three aspects of their relationship with their children (or their co-parenting relationship with their [ex-] partner) that they want to change, and over which they have some control.

The 'Setting goals with parents' worksheet asks the parents to think about where they are now with this aspect of their parenting, where they would ideally like to be, and what would be a realistic goal – say within the next few months. When discussing their answers, you can also ask the parents to consider the following questions:

Why are these important to me?

What do these goals say about the kind of parent I want to be?

And for each goal:

How will I know I've achieved this goal?

What kind of things will I notice in myself and those around me that will tell me I have achieved this goal?

These goals should be held in mind by workers throughout the time you are working together, especially at times when the parents are being asked to evaluate their own ways of thinking and acting:

Does this way of thinking or acting take you closer to or further away from these goals?

In later sessions it is helpful to revisit these goals in a more specific, action-oriented way:

What is the goal? I will know I've achieved this goal when…

Why is this important to me?

What is the next step towards this goal?

What might get in the way?

Solutions – what can I do to deal with any obstacles?

What resources do I have?

How will I know when I've achieved this next step?

Setting goals with parents

Choose and label three aspects of your relationship with your children over which you have some control, and think about how you might like these to change.

Then think about three aspects of your co-parenting relationship with your (ex-) partner over which you have some control, and think about how you might like these to change.

Goal 1. . . . .

Where this is currently at, from 1 to 10 (where the higher the numbers, the better things are):

1   2   3   4   5   6   7   8   9   10

Where I would ideally like it to be:

1   2   3   4   5   6   7   8   9   10

What I would realistically be happy with:

1   2   3   4   5   6   7   8   9   10

Goal 2. . . . .

Where this is currently at, from 1 to 10:

1   2   3   4   5   6   7   8   9   10

Where I would ideally like it to be:

1   2   3   4   5   6   7   8   9   10

What I would realistically be happy with:

1   2   3   4   5   6   7   8   9   10

Goal 3. . . . .

Where this is currently at from 1 to 10:

1   2   3   4   5   6   7   8   9   10

Where I would ideally like it to be:

1   2   3   4   5   6   7   8   9   10

What I would realistically be happy with:

1   2   3   4   5   6   7   8   9   10

Safety planning

You might well find that family members remain at risk from someone who may or may not be involved in your intervention. There may be a violent ex-partner around, for example, or an older teenager who poses a risk but can't be brought to the table to discuss this. Where this is the case, safety planning is very important. The purpose of making a safety plan is to anticipate and plan how to deal with any potentially violent situations. For example, in the case of a mum who has left a relationship with a violent ex-partner, this might include safe contact handovers, or a safe way to take any action she's considering, such as raising a specific issue with her ex-partner.

Break it down into steps:

- Given his past use of violence, look at the level of risk.

- When is she likely to be most at risk? What are her worst fears for herself or her children?

- Does she know when it's going to happen? Is there a pattern or signs?

- What does she already do to protect herself and her children? What works?

- Look at the options she has. Can she avoid the situation altogether or use statutory services, school, a friend, neighbours or family to make the situation safer? Would a safe sanctuary in her home, and an injunction or court order help? Help her develop as wide a range of choices as possible.

- Which options would be most realistic for her? What does she see herself actually being able to do? Focus on those.

Children should be included in safety planning once they are old enough. The key priority for them is their own safety and helping them to find support. Discuss with them:

- When do you think you are most likely to get hurt within your family – that's emotionally or physically – the hurts you can see and the hurts you can't?

- Where is the safest place for you to go at these times?

- Do you have any safe way to get help? (Always encourage children to tell – especially if they are told by an adult to keep a secret).

- What helps you feel comforted or start to feel better?

- Who could you talk to about it?

Safety planning where children or young people are being violent

You may also need to help parents plan for their own safety in situations where young people are being violent in the home. The principles for safety planning are the same as those described earlier, but there will need to be a more detailed analysis of the sequence of events leading up to such violence. We have covered this in more detail in Chapter 7, which looks specifically at the problem of violence toward parents.

Working with parents who are angry at 'the system'

It is not unusual for parents to come to us with a powerful sense that they have been treated unfairly and that in one way or another, 'the system is against them'. It is important to put yourself in the parent's shoes and understand the feelings they have when faced with the power of statutory agencies, especially when the huge strain on these agencies means that they sometimes offer an imperfect service. We of course also have to hold in mind that there may be valid concerns about the parent's behaviour. Our experience is that unless such complaints are acknowledged but also contained in some way, they take up large amounts of time and energy that could be spent working more constructively.

The exercise below is a useful way of acknowledging the difficult emotions that parents experience when agencies intervene in their lives, while helping them identify ways to avoid making things worse and to improve their situation.

Exercise – The wall

Aim

- To help parents who are very angry at the child welfare system to begin to focus more constructively back on what is needed from them.

'The wall'[7] is just a visual analogy for the obstacles the parents are experiencing at the moment – especially the things that get in the way of their relationship with their children. You can draw the wall, actually build the wall or just talk about it. Once you've created a visual analogy using this exercise, you will have established a kind of shorthand and can refer back to it later throughout your work:

> What or who are the obstacles between where your lives are now and how you want them to be? (This might, for example, be about what stands between you and your contact with your children). These are the bricks in the wall. Why do people keep the bricks there?

It doesn't matter if the parent ascribes reasonable or unreasonable motivations to social workers, ex-partners, etc. It is OK to have in one brick 'ex-partner who is still angry at me' and in another 'social worker who is racist' – though you will need to flesh out the latter. For example, you could ask, 'So what is it that the social worker might think about all black men – no matter how racist this is – that would make her want to keep you away from your child?', to which the answer might be 'that all black men are dangerous and unreliable'.

When you face this wall how do you feel (e.g. anger, helplessness, shame)?

How might you act when these feelings are strongest? (What are you tempted to do and say?)

What actions would help to dismantle the wall, and which would only serve to strengthen it?

Even if the bricks in the wall all represent other people's resentment and perceived prejudice, you can still ask questions that switch the focus back to how the parent could change their own behaviour in a constructive way – for example, 'How could you make your ex-partner less angry?' or 'How could you show the social worker that this racist stereotype doesn't fit you?'

Any time a parent is tempted to 'bang their head against the wall' again in future, you will be able to refer back to your earlier work on 'the wall' and ask again what sort of behaviour might encourage those who've made the wall to begin dismantling it little by little, rather than building it up.

The intervention stage

By now you should have assessed your family and planned an intervention pathway together.

From here on, this book will take you through a series of techniques and exercises to help you work in a structured and focused way with the parents.

4 Child Discipline

This chapter provides some basic material on generally improving the quality of the parent–child relationship and child discipline. This is the sort of territory covered by most parenting programmes. It will be helpful for a parent who is basically competent and confident to decide what behaviours need management.

However, before doing this work with parents, take note of where you feel the parents fit on the continuum of parenting we outlined in the first chapter. You can teach these techniques, but if the parents' ability to set and protect their own boundaries is damaged, if they feel terrified of their child, or if they feel very guilty, then they simply won't be able to use them. Conversely, with over-authoritarian parents, the place to start may not be in providing them with behaviour management techniques but in increasing their empathy and attunement with their child, and raising their awareness that over-harsh discipline is likely to be both damaging and counter-productive.

✎ Exercise – What counts as abuse?

This is a 'quiz', which is designed to instigate discussion of abuse – it can be used with a family or group, or with parents alone.

Aim

- To encourage critical thinking about what is abusive, especially about issues of power, intention and context.

Give each person the worksheet 'What counts as abuse?'

Ask everyone to privately consider which of the behaviours are abusive, and then to discuss their answers and their reasoning.

There is no right and wrong answer, but the discussion may help parents clarify where they feel a line should be drawn between what is and is not OK within their family.

What counts as abuse?

- Smacking a 3-year-old for running on the road.

- Smacking an 8-year-old for not being able to read.

- A 10-year-old boy giving his 12-year-old brother a black eye in a fight.

- A 10-year-old giving his 4-year-old brother a black eye in a fight.

- A baby biting his mother.

- A 12-year-old biting his mother.

- A mother biting her baby.

- A 10-year-old saying, 'I hate you!' to a parent.

- A parent saying, 'I hate you!' to a 10-year-old.

Undermining shame and fear-based methods of discipline and defining child-centred methods

✐ Exercise – Discipline
Aims

- To establish a pattern for parents of thinking of their long-term learning goals for their children rather than simply what behaviours they want to manage in the here-and-now.

- To define shame and fear-based discipline methods versus child-centred methods.

- To discourage shame and fear-based discipline by showing that in the long term such methods will not work, because children mainly learn not to get caught.

- To show how shame and fear-based discipline will damage the development of autonomous value judgement, emotional regulation and self-esteem in their children.

Point out that 'discipline' is related to the word 'disciple' – someone who learns from another person.

Ask the parents how they want their children to turn out:

If the discipline/teaching works, what sort of things will your children have learned? What kind of people might we hope they will grow up to be?

What characteristics do you want to see in them as they become independent people in the world?

What would you see in them that would give you the confidence that they can live well without you?

List the answers that the parents give.

If the term 'respect' arises, make sure it is clearly defined:

The term 'respect' is used in a range of ways. Do you mean that you want them to do what people say out of fear and obedience, or do you mean that you would like them to admire positive behaviours and be polite?

Example answers – characteristics you want to foster in your children in the long term: happy, self-controlled, good values, kind, polite, successful, good self-esteem, etc.

Explain to the parents that some forms of discipline work by shaming and scaring children into changing their behaviour. See if you can list as many examples of these between you as possible.

Example answers – shame and fear-based discipline: smacking, name calling, labelling, threatening, screaming at a child.

Ask the parents if they think these forms of discipline work in the short term (probably many of them do – it's a point for a brief discussion).

Ask the parents whether these methods are likely to contribute positively towards the characteristics they want to foster in their children in the long term. (*Note:* Some will but most won't).

Work through the exercise on impacts of shaming and put-downs and the handout 'Problems with physical punishment of children'.

✎ Exercise – Impacts of shaming and put-downs

Let the parents share ways they remember being put down or felt they were negatively labelled as children.

> How did this affect you?
>
> How did you feel about the person who said those things to you?
>
> How do you do that to your own child?
>
> How can you praise your own child – both for specific skills and attributes but also for specific behaviours?

Introduce the concept of child-centred discipline in contrast to shame and fear-based discipline. Explain:

> We call 'child-centred parenting' the kind of methods that really do teach children to grow into the kind of people who can be happy, functioning individuals with values and the ability to consider and discern right and wrong for themselves.
>
> Shame and fear-based methods (smacking, shouting, shutting in room) teach children to fear getting caught and often have long-term negative consequences for their self-esteem, their ability to make their own moral judgements and their ability to form healthy relationships.

✎ Exercise – The idea of child-centred parenting: establishing a principle to guide our parenting

By child-centred parenting, we mean teaching a child:

- only what it is in the child's interests to learn
- by using methods that best serve the child's long-term interests.

Start the session by getting a rich description of what this looks like by eliciting examples of ways to be child centred in your parenting. (It is important to get examples of how we treat the other parent as well as the child). Then ask for ways we might behave towards our children, or towards the other parent, that would fall at the other end of the 'Parenting continuum' (see Figure 4.1).[8]

Note that child-centred parenting usually takes patience and time and effort (modelling, teaching, discussing, explaining, listening, convincing, involving) while parent-centred methods involve quick easy wins (smacking, shouting, shutting in room). On the other hand, parent-centred methods usually teach children to fear getting caught doing the undesired behaviour, while child-centred methods are aimed at getting children to internalise values in the longer term along with the ability to assess right or wrong for themselves rather than blindly obeying rules.

Child-centred

Gives lots of positive reinforcement
Provides stimulating activities and interactions with the child
Makes clear and simple rules to keep the child safe and healthy
Occasionally tells the child off or stops them doing dangerous or hurtful things
Is respectful of the other parent
Listens to their child
Communicates about sexuality and healthy relationships
Notices and meets the child's needs

Parent-centred

Insults child, uses put-downs
Only expresses conditional love and ambivalent feelings to child
Uses harsh or cruel control methods
Is neglectful
Shows no sensitivity to child's needs
Acts in ways which frighten, threaten or provoke
Is unpredictable depending on how they feel
Uses coercion, threats or bribes
Is sexually or physically coercive
Puts down, abuses or is violent to the other parent

Figure 4.1 Parenting continuum

Problems with physical punishment of children

- It teaches children that violence can be used to control other people – and a big problem with this is that a lot of them start to use violence themselves to solve conflicts or else find it normal and acceptable when other people bully them.

- Hitting children tends to make them angrier. Anger becomes a way of being in the world and may contribute to children being rebellious, violent or aggressive.

- Children learn to fear those they love, and love those they should fear. This may lead them to choose violent partners and friends.

- People who are hit often end up feeling very ashamed and feeling badly about themselves – with negative effects on their self-esteem.

- Many children nowadays view being hit as an infringement of their rights – and resent it. What's more, if a child focuses on the injustice of a person's actions, this can actually take the focus off what the child has done. The bad behaviour is forgotten and the child is more likely to feel anger than guilt.

- As children grow, it becomes increasingly hard for mum to impose the same kind of discipline as dad. The old cry of 'Wait till your father gets home!' is not a healthy one. Dad will become the disciplinarian ogre while mum loses respect because she cannot control the kids. This will of course have huge ramifications if you separate.

- Eventually your children will become teenagers and will outgrow the ability of both of you to overpower them. As children outgrow physical punishment, it can be difficult switching to other methods of discipline.

- Children in some families set each other up for punishment by the adults – sometimes quite skilfully. They are more likely to get a kick out of this if physical punishment is being meted out.

- Hitting out is often more a short-term emotional release for an adult and is thus not used consistently or predictably. Children may learn to see it more as an indicator of a person's mood than as an indicator that they have done something wrong.

- Because many parents feel guilty or embarrassed about using physical punishment, they often give mixed messages to children and are less likely to be consistent.

- As it is now frowned upon in public, some children will deliberately act up when they know a parent can't hit them.

- For some adults, the use of physical punishment makes physical abuse much more likely. It's one thing to say that you are very thoughtful and controlled about the way you use smacking but another to be that careful when you're feeling really wound up with your child.

- Families have got into serious strife when a child is accidentally injured when being hit or trying to avoid being hit.

- Some children start to hit back when they are big enough.

- You can't say, 'We don't hit in this family', when your children are violent.

- Parents seldom agree about physical punishment and are less likely to work together. Also children play on the sympathy of the other parent.

- Some children may come to think it is all rather amusing: getting you to chase them around the house in impotent rage.

- Most parents report that it doesn't actually work very well.

(Adapted from the work of Eddie Gallagher).

Steps for child-centred behaviour management

The important thing about the following strategies is that they are steps like rungs on a ladder. You have to achieve Step 1 before going to Step 2 and so on. So, for instance, you can't use time-outs without trying all the previous steps. This also means that you don't get out the big guns for the small problems and blow all your tricks at once. If you do this, you will only devalue your discipline techniques by over-using them.

Step 1 – Modelling

This is the way we pick up most of what we learn about relationships and how to be in the world. It's vital not to use violence and put-downs if you expect your children to do the same. It's equally vital that we show our children how to keep firm boundaries if we expect them to learn how to do so.

Ask the parent:

> Who is important in your child's life?
>
> What behaviours from you set good examples of how to communicate with these people, set boundaries with them, stay safe and manage frustration?
>
> How do you rate yourself on a scale of 1 to 10 in communicating (where 1 is 'really bad at this' and 10 is 'perfect'), setting boundaries, staying safe and managing frustration with others – especially those important to your child?
>
> How can you be positive to your child about others who are important in your child's life without being dishonest (e.g. other parent, foster carers, etc.)?

Step 2 – Giving clear instructions

Explain that parents need to give clear instructions as to what they want children to do. 'Be good at Nan's' is too vague. 'Help Nan by washing and drying up all the pots, pans and plates after dinner. Get into bed by 11 without making her have to tell you, and don't read or keep the light on any later than 11.30' is better.

For younger children, you couldn't expect them to retain so many instructions so you would have to choose the most important single specific instruction – say, 'Go to bed as soon as Nan tells you to without arguing.'

Step 3 – Giving praise and attention for good behaviour

It might be worthwhile getting parents to log the praise they give to their children. Encourage them to notice what the child does, and praise specific achievements. There is a danger that, if you tell children who feel badly about themselves that they are good, or clever, they may find this hard to take on board or believe.

Model this yourself by praising the things parents are doing that show you that they love and care for their children. If you haven't already done the work on family strengths or the worksheet 'Positive regard for my child', then now is the time.

Step 4 – Ignoring some bad behaviour

Many of the parents you work with will find this extremely hard. Even where they agree to ignore some behaviours, you should run through with them how this will work in practice and get them to think about the feelings this may evoke in them. For example, if they decide to ignore tantrums, how will they do this – where will they go and what will they do, and what if the child ups the stakes? Or what if they ask the child to do something and the child says no? How will they let this go?

You may need to suggest that parents ask for cooperation rather than demand obedience around some issues (see the next exercise) so that it's easier for them to let go of it if the child does not agree to do what they want.

You may also need to discuss the commonly held idea that, if you give an inch with children, they will take a mile. Is this true? Or do you just get into huge battles about small issues and exhaust yourselves?

✎ Exercise – What can be ignored

This exercise will help you to explore with parents which of their children's behaviours it is possible, or desirable, to ignore.

Divide a page into columns headed 'Behaviour I want to encourage' and 'Behaviour I want to discourage' and list these together. Then, for the behaviours the parents want to discourage, mark out those that they feel cannot be ignored – first those that are safety issues in red, then in another colour mark those that can't be ignored because they are important to the parents.

You might want to discuss the importance a parent assigns to these behaviours – are these received ideas that the parent has given little thought to? What would actually happen if they were ignored? Might it be enough to encourage change through praising and rewarding an alternative, and ignoring the negative behaviour at least in the short term?

From this exercise, you should become clearer about what can be ignored at least for an agreed period. (Contract with parents for them to try ignoring and praising for a month, and then review the effects).

Step 5 – Confrontation

This involves saying 'NO, don't do that' followed by firm authoritative instructions – it's important to note that this is about parents getting their child's attention and showing they are serious – not about releasing anger and frustration by ranting or yelling.

Step 6 – Incentives

Star charts work for younger children – set them up for a limited number of specific agreed behaviours (no more than three at a time) and maintain them consistently until better habits have formed.

Incentives charts work on older children with agreed rewards when the child has earned enough points from agreed 'goal' behaviours.

✎ Exercise – Setting up an incentives chart

Help parents manage the maths on this.

1. List goal behaviours (as many as you like) and the number of times per week the young person might achieve each of these.

2. Figure out the rewards and how often the parent could afford or manage to offer these (they may be treats for all the family, time spent together, increased access to computer or TV, etc., buying stuff for the young person, letting them choose where to go on holiday, letting them have friends stay over or whatever).

3. Calculate the rewards for each good behaviour based on

   high achieving week = max rewards possible.

These reward schemes mean that the parents don't punish the undesired behaviour any more – only reward the good. This may substantially diminish the feeling of living in a battleground.

Step 7 – Consequences

Offer choices and speak of the natural consequences first (e.g. 'If you make the choice to wear only a t-shirt when you go out, then you will end up feeling cold.'). However, for many children immediate gratification, such as getting a packet of sweets, will tend to outweigh long-term consequences such as the danger of having to go to the dentist in the future.

For this kind of issue, you can try setting consequences that are as logical as possible (e.g. 'I won't buy biscuits unless you brush your teeth') – but this isn't always easy and you may simply have to set otherwise illogical negative consequences for bad behaviours (e.g. the confiscation of toys for younger children).

There are several important things to bear in mind when discussing consequences with parents – for example,

- How comfortable are you, and your partner, about using such a consequence? If you are going to be more inconvenienced than the child, then it is not likely to work.

- Is the consequence too over the top to be applied as frequently as the unwanted behaviour warrants?

- Does the child or young person care about it sufficiently for it to be a deterrent? It's helpful to get the young person's input on what seems the right level of consequence for a given behaviour.

- How consistently can you apply the consequence? We like to tell children the story of the boy who cried wolf, but the same applies to parents. If you make a threat and don't follow it through, your child will cease to believe you and your word will very quickly lose its power.

- Negative consequences should be short term – they should be done and dusted in 24 hours.

- If the consequence needs cooperation from the young person – for example grounding them – be sure there is sufficient compliance to make it stick. You need to work out consequences that you can control. You can then use these to encourage cooperation with time-outs, grounding, extra chores, etc.

EXAMPLES

If you choose not to go to time-out, you have no electronics (TV, computer, game-boy) for the rest of the day. Your choice.

Last time we sent you to bed early, you chose not to cooperate. You can choose to go to bed early or, if you would rather, you can lose the use of your bike for one day for every hour you are up past eight.

If you choose not to cooperate with being grounded, you will lose all privileges, which means no TV, computer, snacks, lifts, telephone, etc. for twice as long as the grounding.

Some parents will need to set up a consistent system for giving first, in order to have the possibility of taking away. Giving regular treats, privileges and pocket money allows parents to make children pay for breakages or thefts and can even be used to fine for bad behaviours. Lots of parents live somewhat chaotically and give treats and privileges based on whims or their own circumstances, thereby radically limiting their options in terms of setting consequences. They will need to consider what they can make regular – options go well beyond the purely financial to other kinds of privileges such as luxury or sweet food, going out, having friends over, access to cars, TVs, phones and computers.

Whether parents are aware of it or not, they will be doing much more for their children than they may realise (e.g. cooking, cleaning, washing clothes). In more risky situations where parents are not willing to allow any choice, they may insist that the children must first do X before they will do anything more for them in any way at all.

✎ Exercise – Using consequences

This exercise aims to teach realistic and effective ways of using consequences.

Divide a page into four areas and get the parents to answer the following:

What behaviour do you need to reduce or eliminate (especially abusive or self-destructive behaviours)?

What behaviour do you merely wish to discourage (such as annoying habits)?

What behaviour can you ignore for now?

What behaviour do you want to encourage?

Say to the parents: 'Be clear about your priorities. Whether or not teenagers do their homework is not currently very important if they are also abusing you and abusing drugs. Choose your battles carefully.'

✎ Exercise – What consequences do parents have at their disposal?

Ask the parents to make an inventory of all they do for their children. This should span:

- all the things they pay for, including treats (e.g. going out, bicycles, trainers) and non-vital things for daily life (e.g. sweets, haircuts, clothes, telephone bills)

- all the services they perform, such as driving their children around, cooking for them and cleaning

- all the privileges they allow them, such as going out or having friends over, using computers, TVs, staying up late, sleeping in late, playing their music, using make-up, using phones, taking part in activities and so on.

Discuss how these could be made regular and whether they could be used as consequences for unwanted behaviours. (Parents should not stop providing basic needs such as shelter, food, clothing and love, or privileges that contribute to a child's personal growth, such as music lessons, athletic activities, youth club or scouts. However, crisps and sweets aren't basic needs and playing computer games or going to a party with friends aren't growth activities).

Step 8 – Time-out

Time-out should not be an alternative to completing a task, but a consequence of bad behaviour.

5 Working with Parents on the Impact of Domestic Violence on Their Children

When working with parents who have perpetrated violence in the home, it is important to raise their awareness of the many negative effects that growing up with violence and abuse can have on children.

This can be done by direct teaching (see the section on 'Explaining the impacts of domestic violence on children') but we've also provided tools to take it a bit deeper by using the more interactive and experiential exercises contained in this chapter. However, it is important to note that there will be a different emphasis when working with perpetrators and victims.

Perpetrators of domestic violence

Many perpetrators of domestic violence are caught up in resentment and anger towards their partners and block out any awareness of the harm they have done to them. However, it is our experience that they may be less shut off from the possibility of admitting that exposure to violence and conflict is harmful to their children. First, most parents are likely to agree that severe conflict between parents hurts children, regardless of the 'rights and wrongs' of the disputes between the adults. Whether or not they are willing to admit this, it is likely that the parents will remember particular instances when their children were present during violent incidents. Also, many of the people we work with are likely to remember such incidents in their own childhoods, and their discomfort at these memories can be an important point of entry for discussions about how they want to be as a parent. It is also important to acknowledge that the fact that the parent has taken the trouble to meet with you is a powerful indicator that they want to ensure a different future for their own children.

However, parents are likely to start out by minimising the extent to which their children were exposed to violence and conflict, because of how difficult it can be to contemplate that a child may have suffered fear, distress or emotional harm as a result of one's actions. It is, for instance, very common for parents to state categorically that their children were never present when the violence happened. The aim of the teaching and exercises in this section is to start to reduce this minimisation. However, there is a delicate balance to be drawn here. An insensitive and accusing approach to this topic could lead to abusive parents feeling shamed and moving away from feelings of empathy for their children into angry dismissal and externalisation of blame.

The non-abusive parent

When working with victims of domestic violence, there is a different balance to be held. It is important not to minimise the effects of exposure to violence on children, because this can be a powerful motivating factor for women to seek help or to end a violent relationship. The realisation that the violence is affecting the children, or the time when the perpetrator threatens or carries out harm to a child, is often the 'tipping point' that leads a woman to take decisive action. However, it is also important to acknowledge the huge barriers to leaving a violent relationship, and to enquire about and validate the many ways in which the parent has acted in the past to protect her children from the violence.

✎ Exercise – Icebergs

If you are working with children, explain how most of an iceberg is hidden beneath the water. Draw this on a sheet of paper.

Ask the children what they show when their mum and dad fight. What would be visible in terms of their actions and feelings? Draw or write this into the visible section of the iceberg.

Then ask them what they don't show, and what lies underneath the surface. Draw or write this into the submerged section of the iceberg.

With parents, ask them to draw their child's iceberg – 'What does he or she show on the surface when these things go on?', and 'What do you imagine is going on underneath?'

Ask the parents to look at what their child has drawn and then show them another iceberg.

Say: 'When you look at what your child has drawn, these are the things *you* show on the surface' and write in what you see. Then hand the pen to each parent and ask: 'What's going on underneath for you?'

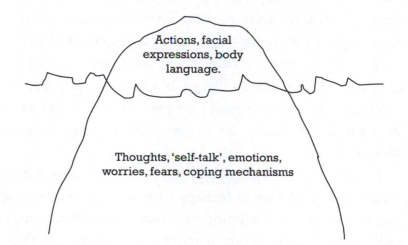

Actions, facial expressions, body language.

Thoughts, 'self-talk', emotions, worries, fears, coping mechanisms

Figure 5.1 The iceberg

Explaining the impacts of domestic violence on children

There are many ways that domestic violence can have an impact on children. This book is not intended to cover these issues theoretically but instead to help professionals explain some of these impacts to the parents they are working with. What follows is therefore a very simple description of the mechanisms by which domestic violence affects children from birth onwards. Choose the explanations that fit your case rather than going through them all with the parent/s.

The effects of scary and traumatic events on very young babies and on the unborn child

This is most important to explain to parents where:

- the domestic violence was going on when the child was in utero or in the first two years of life and

- the child is now showing poor concentration/has been diagnosed with attention deficit hyperactivity disorder (ADHD)/seems very fearful/is quick to anger/is very frozen/desensitised.

Human beings are born 'undercooked' compared with many other mammals. We are very dependent on our parents for a much longer period than other animals, some of whom hit the ground and almost immediately start walking about. This 'half-cookedness' goes beyond the physical development of the human baby and is also true in terms of our brain development. The hard-wiring of our brains is still forming in the first 18 months of life, and the brain circuits and systems are being shaped by early experiences. The systems that are most used at that time become the most emphasised and most active thereafter. This includes our overall stress-response system, which includes the basic 'flight-fight-freeze' responses to threatening events.

We can imagine the baby being born, and, like all animals, scanning the environment for potential threats. If a baby is repeatedly frightened or exposed to shocks, the stress response system can end up becoming over-active, with the result that the baby can become frozen, jumpy or seem angry and hard to manage.

In schoolchildren the jumpiness and poor concentration can often lead to a diagnosis of ADHD. In teenagers we see that some young people have lower 'stimulus-response thresholds' than others. Some get much angrier at seemingly small provocations, or are much more nervous and fearful. Their adrenalin seems to be pumping already in situations where others may still feel calm. This makes it harder for them to deal with anger without hitting out. But of course, although it is hard, they can learn to calm themselves down or to express their anger in other ways.

The effects of domestic violence on infants and on the development of their ways of bonding in close relationships (attachment styles)

This is most important to explain to parents where:

- the domestic violence was happening when the child was an infant from 0 to 3 years old or where it persisted for many years and

- the child appears very needy, clingy and hard to comfort or is very cut off and over-independent.

Our attachment style is the way we bond with and relate to very close others – like parents and, later on in life, girlfriends and boyfriends. It seems that we all develop a pattern or template for this in the first two years of life and that it is based largely on the relationship we had then with our main carer (usually our mum).

Note: This is a way to give a simple and graphic explanation of this important idea – a sort of *Blue Peter* demonstration of attachment theory. You'll need a jug of water, a drip tray of some sort, a couple of bits of cling film and two plastic cups – one perforated with little holes.

Explain to the parent you are working with that the jug represents the mother and the cup represents the baby. The baby has many needs and discomforts that cause it to cry. Mum tries to meet the baby's needs and when she gets it right (e.g. by giving a hungry baby a feed) the baby is sated and stops crying. It feels understood and satisfied. We can say that an amount of 'loving-kindness-security' has gone from mother to baby. And, of course, the cessation of crying is a big relief to mum, who feels validated as a result. In this way, some of the loving-kindness has passed back from baby to her.

To demonstrate this, say that the water represents this 'loving-kindness-security', and pour a bit from the jug to the cup and then a part of that back again from cup to jug as you move through the narrative; demonstrate the various stages by pouring water back and forth, or spilling it at the appropriate times.

Over time and with these repeated interactions, baby gets more and more full of security and loving kindness, which continues to pass to and fro between baby and mum. Scary events, like falling over, can make a little bit spill out but baby learns that mum will quickly be there to offer comfort and top up the loving-kindness-security again. Eventually, the baby's expectation of receiving comfort when it is needed, and the sense of being full enough of good stuff to risk a little spill here and there, serve to form a safe base. This sense of security allows the infant to venture further and further from mum and out into the world.

This way of relating in which both people are open to the other's love and comfort, but also 'full enough' to feel secure and to move away for periods to explore the world, is called *secure attachment*. Some boyfriends and girlfriends operate in a similar way – they can show and meet each other's neediness but are also pretty secure and outward-facing much of the time.

In those early years it's fine for mum not to always immediately meet her baby's needs. She can afford to get it wrong sometimes, or take her time to get it right sometimes, so long as she then comforts the baby and 'repairs' the baby's distress. She only needs to get it right around half of the time for secure attachment to result.

But when very frightening things happen, like a violent argument, a lot of the security is spilled out. This is when the baby has a huge need for comfort, and when baby's attachment needs are highest. If mum or dad respond in a frightened or frightening way (like they might in the middle of a heated scary row), this doesn't have to happen very often to damage the secure attachment. Unable to bear the high level of non-comforted distress, no longer safe in the knowledge that what is spilled will be quickly replaced, babies have to find their own way to get and hold some securing loving-kindness.

One choice is to hold in whatever is left there to protect their soft and vulnerable insides – this is like putting cling film over the cup (put a piece of cling film over the cup to demonstrate). But now it is harder for baby to take in love – he or she is too defensive. And so it is harder for mum's love to go in and for baby's love to come back. This is painful for mum too, and she may little by little close off herself also (demonstrate this by also covering the jug with cling film). Mum will experience this as a difficulty in bonding with her child and it also may make her feel very guilty. This is called *avoidant attachment*. 'Avoidant' kids don't seem so affected by the traumas around them. They may be watching TV or playing while arguments rage between their parents. People often feel reassured by this but these children may develop into adults who can't easily accept love and comfort or allow themselves to be close to or show their needs to others. In relationships they often feel their space being infringed upon and want their girlfriend or boyfriend to back off. They may find other people's needs hard to tolerate – even their own children's neediness.

Another choice a baby has to get more loving-kindness is to become more open – more porous. That way that baby can soak up good attention from everywhere (equivalent to perforating a cup). But of course when love is received it can't really be held onto – the baby leaks security (pour water into the leaky cup to demonstrate). This is called *anxious attachment*. He or she is clingy, very hard to comfort and very distressed when separated from mum but also may be very open to affection from anyone – even relative strangers. As adults, anxiously attached people are needy, very nervous about their partners leaving them and often quite jealous and 'co-dependent'. They tend to be very 'inward-facing' in their relationships.

Most difficult as an attachment style is actually a mixture of both these – called *disorganised attachment*. The baby can be too 'leaky' at moments and too closed off at others. Not only can loving-kindness hardly get in but, if it does, it is hard for baby to hold onto. Children with disorganised attachment may grow up to have real problems with relationships later because they both fear abandonment and get jealous, at the same time as being unable to bear it when their girlfriend or boyfriend gets too close. They constantly feel the need to pull their partner closer then push them away.

Many of us grow up with some degree of anxious or avoidant attachment in our way of relating to others. But repeated exposure to domestic violence can cause children to develop more extreme versions of these styles of relating. And we need to know that, if our children are already showing signs of one of these, then:

- it is possible to turn it around

- but it isn't quick to turn it around, particularly the older and more 'hard-wired' the child.

You can demonstrate how a parent may have to do a lot of 'pouring' love and comfort into the child without much coming back (here make a little hole in the cling film over the cup and try to pour water from the jug into it – not a lot goes in, and none comes back) – before the avoidant child begins to take down its defences (gradually expand the hole in the cling film so more water goes in) or the anxious child starts to shore up its boundaries (here wrap some cling film round the perforated cup so it holds water). Only then will mum and dad get much back for their efforts. And it can really take years of painstaking loving despite no apparent changes before you get there (experts tell us to expect two to five years).

The effects of domestic violence on what children learn about the way the world works

Explain that by witnessing domestic violence, children can learn that it is a normal or acceptable way to settle conflicts, and that if you aren't the abuser you will be the abused. Those of us who learn this might 'kick off' whenever we feel angry or are involved in a disagreement. Some of us end up being victims ourselves later and thinking this is normal. Others of us again learn that conflict is dangerous – potentially catastrophic – and we avoid it at all costs throughout life, trying over-hard to please others.

Children also absorb their knowledge of relationships from seeing how their mum and dad behave with each other.

For a parent discussing domestic violence with children, it is important not to make light of the abuse in any way, and not to make excuses (e.g. 'Daddy is ill'). Parents need to explain that the abuse was wrong and serious. Equally, parents need to understand clearly and explain to the children that exposing them to ongoing violence is also emotional abuse of them. Even if abused parents are struggling to prioritise their own safety, they do not have the right to impose domestic violence on their children. Parents should encourage their children to be clear about the boundaries they should set in life and expect others to respect.

The effects of domestic violence on family dynamics

These are important to explain to parents where:

- the abused party, compared with the abuser, is struggling to set boundaries.

Domestic violence distorts families. Triangle 1 is an ideal family power structure – it doesn't matter if mum and dad are together or not, but they are both equal in power and above the children.

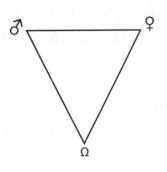

Figure 5.2 Triangle 1

Domestic violence skews this (Triangle 2) so that the violent partner has more power than the other parent who may be barely above the children in the power relationship – sometimes even below (Triangle 3).

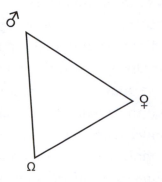

Figure 5.3 Triangle 2

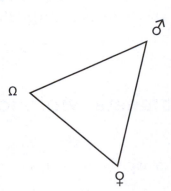

Figure 5.4 Triangle 3

This might be because the children join in with the abuse. The abuser is, after all, the most important one in the family to please and be on the right side of. Plus the abuser may also be much more 'together' than the victim, who is being undermined and destabilised all the time. It can get to the stage where the victimised parent is so broken down by the abuse that even the youngest children start trying to comfort and protect her. She becomes so disempowered by the abuse and they become so parent-like that the parent–child relationship turns upside down.

In such cases it is important for the victims to take back a positive parenting role in the family and for their partners and children to give up power themselves, and to support the victims in reasserting themselves.

Children learn self-care, self-respect and boundary setting from their parents' modelling. It is definitely possible for victims who feel guilty about their children being exposed to domestic violence to be too child focused, just as it is possible for abusing parents to go too far in the other direction.

However, you can't make it up to your children by being soft – they need clear boundaries and firm consequences. Parents need to understand their children's behaviour but also to deal with it regardless of where it stems from.

Previously abused parents should model not accepting abuse from anyone – including their kids. If younger children see an older brother or sister abusing a parent and there are no consequences, they are more likely to copy this behaviour. It is important for there to be consequences even if these appear (in the short term) to have no effect whatsoever on the abusive child.

Resilience

While it is vital for parents to be aware that living with conflict and aggression is harmful to children, there is a danger that, if we focus solely on the harm caused, we may foster a sense of hopelessness and a belief that their children's lives have been damaged beyond repair. This could lead to parents feeling powerless to bring about positive changes in their children's lives. The truth is that, while the children will definitely be affected by exposure to domestic violence, many children who grow up in very difficult circumstances go on to have happy and productive lives. There has also been a lot of research on the factors that help children through difficult times. The most important message is that, once the abuse stops, the healing can start.

Things that help children come through the experience well, despite having lived with domestic violence, are:

- parents being insistent that they don't argue or have serious discussions when the children are around

- contact with lots of supportive adults who know about what has happened and will offer love

- permission (especially from parents) to talk to others freely

- contact with peers who've gone through similar things

- the best possible relationship from now on with both parents

- parents who, if separated, can manage a functioning relationship (not necessarily friendship)

- anything that increases their self-esteem – extra-curricular activities, running clubs, drama shows, etc.

- getting therapy or specialist help to understand and express themselves better – or just have someone to talk to where they don't have to be 'diplomatic'

- mum and dad giving them a clear explanation of what happened and why – with no excuses

- mum and dad getting support to understand and parent the kids

- helping others through voluntary work, mentoring, etc.

- having a safety plan so they have some control over their safety if domestic violence happens again.

Building child empathy

On the whole, people find it very hard to acknowledge the impact that the domestic violence has had on their children. This is understandable – none of us wants to think of our children suffering and the additional guilt from feeling that this may be linked more or less directly with our own choices or actions can make it hard to bear. As a result, parents can be in a great deal of denial about their children's experience. Increasing their felt empathy can be a useful additional step to simply educating them (as through the previous didactic section of this chapter). Increasing parents' ability to really feel for the effects on their children can increase their motivation to safeguard the children and prioritise their needs in future.

Parents stop themselves empathising partly in order to avoid guilt, and it's important to remember that, while guilt can be highly motivating, it can also be very incapacitating at a level where it becomes overwhelming. Always have in your mind that you want parents to feel the scale of the problem, and to be thinking of themselves as the solution. Most especially if they were the victims of the abuse, you will need to actively discourage them from seeing themselves as the cause. There is some specific work you can do around this issue that you may want to use in conjunction with empathy-building work (see Chapter 3 on building strengths and Chapter 8 for the exercises 'Is it all my fault?' and 'Exploring guilt and shame').

If you do decide it might be productive to gently begin to dismantle some of the parents' barriers to empathy, a useful way to start is to get them connecting to their own childhood feelings of powerlessness and then linking these to their children's experiences.

Ask about their own parents' fighting and arguing

Just get them to describe what they were aware of and how they got to be aware of these things. In particular, establish whether or not their parents knew the full extent of how much their children were aware of the arguments between them. In general, children's awareness usually far exceeds what their parents think. Once you've established that, you can come back to it later to help them think about their own children's awareness.

It may also be helpful to go more deeply into their childhood experience of hearing their parents argue. You might ask: 'So you were a little kid and your parents would argue – where were you? Would you tell me a bit about what you heard and saw?'

There are a number of ways to deepen your clients' connections to their painful childhood feelings that you might want to use – but only if they seem very cut off from these:

1. Use empathy yourself to acknowledge and enhance your clients' feelings – for example, 'that sounds terrifying.'

2. Use visual memory – for example, 'What are you seeing in your mind's eye when you think of that? Picturing yourself as that powerless little child, what do you see on her face? What is she feeling? My guess is she is thinking…and feeling… Is that close?'

3. Explore their isolation – for example, 'Who stood by you and helped you back then? Who did you talk to about it? What stopped you telling more people? What did you imagine they'd think of you?'

Link this back to their children's experience

Ask your clients if they imagine any differences for their own children's experience (allowing them to voice and somewhat free themselves from their defences first) and then about any similarities there may be. Explore the similarities further – for example, 'And if you picture her like that – feeling some of those things and terrified – what do you feel then? What are you realising when you try to picture that?'

Add some motivational questions

There's no point in doing this session at all if it simply leaves parents ashamed and depressed. It's important that they can see why and how to harness their learning to help their own children. There are a couple of suggestions that you can pull in if you see your clients are slipping into shame or are simply unable to see the point in all this.

Do acknowledge the connection between your clients' defensiveness, guilt and shame and their care for their child – if they didn't care, they wouldn't feel bad talking about all this. For example, 'I can see that's hard to do right. What sort of person would you be if it wasn't hard/if you didn't feel that? In some ways the discomfort you feel thinking about this is direct evidence of your love for your children.'

Another way to help your clients make use of looking through this window to empathy is to help them understand the benefits of doing so for their children. For example:

Did either of your parents ever think of you this way?

What difference might it have made if they had really stopped and pictured you like you did with your children?

Did anyone even try to hold the person who abused you to account?

That's incredibly unfair – it's unfair expecting you to think this way about your children when no-one made your abuser/s think this way about you.

But it also says something about you that you're talking to me like this.

You could have come here and said nothing.

What does it say about you?

Who knows that about you?

Is that something about you that's really different from your abuser?

✏ Exercise – Child empathy role play

This exercise takes the one before a stage further. It is primarily for using with the adult domestic violence perpetrator because it has a strong emotional impact and there's a danger that, if it is used with the adult domestic violence victim, it will be inappropriately guilt inducing.

Start by saying that it's often difficult to really hold your children in mind and understand their experience, especially at times when we are caught up in angry disputes with our partners. Explain to the parents that this exercise is a way of using their imagination to put themselves as much as possible into their children's shoes.

Ask the parent if he is willing to play the role of his child.

Reassure the parent that you're not expecting to get an accurate version of what the child really thinks or feels – just to get him to say what he imagines his child would say. Take care to point out that this is all we can possibly get at and say that, if he feels he doesn't know the answer to a question, just to improvise and guess – it's surprising what he may find he has insight into.

To get him into role, ask him to sit in a different chair, to sit as the child might sit and to give some personal information relating to the child. Ask for a description of the child, and ask a few other questions such as 'What's your (the child's) favourite TV programme? What's your (the child's) favourite game?'

Then go on to use the suggested interview questions loosely. Stick with eliciting feelings rather than facts. The object is to get the parent feeling for their child. Don't get into safety planning, problem solving or trying to make the child feel better – remember this is not a real child. For each question you ask about what happened, ask another about what that was like for the child and how it felt.

After the role play, be sure to de-role the parent again. This involves getting him to agree that he is no longer playing the role of his child, and to talk about the ways he differs from his child. Ask one or two questions to get him 'back to himself', such as 'What's the first thing you'd do if you won the Lottery?' Allow time for him to say what the exercise was like for him.

You can do a version of this that feels less like role play although it will be harder for the parent to get the same level of insight into the young person. Rather than getting him into role, simply ask, 'What would you guess (your child) might say if I asked…?'

Some parents simply won't be able to manage this exercise at all, or empathise with their children. In this case, simply point out how hard the exercise is and explore with them why it is important that a parent should be able to imagine what their child is feeling; then go on to use less experiential and more educational techniques to help them to understand their children's experience.

Suggested interview questions

- What do you like best about your dad?
- Tell me about a special memory you have of your dad.
- What are your earliest memories of your mum and dad arguing?
- Where were you?
- What did do you do?
- That sounds really scary – what did you think when that was going on?
- Who did you tell about it?
- Why didn't you tell more people?
- What did you fear they might think?
- How do you think things might have been different with your friends and family, etc., if you didn't have this secret?
- How do you know an argument is brewing in your house?
- What's been the scariest time?
- Where were you?

- What did you do?

- How did you feel?

- What was going through your head at that time?

- Did you feel differently after that?

- Did you feel differently about yourself/your mum/your dad/your brothers and sisters?

- What happened afterwards?

- Who comforted you?

- Why do you think he does it?

- What's it like not knowing why he's doing this?

- What do you start to say about yourself?

- Is he too strict with you?

- When does he scare you?

- How do you deal with that?

- How do you think all this affects you?

- How have you come to cope with this?

- Is there a downside to your coping mechanism?

- Can you tell your dad how you feel?

- Why not?

- What sort of relationship do you want with your dad?

- If you could say one thing to him here and now, what would it be?

Increasing a child's resilience by encouraging contact with significant others

Both victims and abusers are likely to minimise the many effects of growing up around domestic violence, because of how difficult and hurtful it can be to contemplate that their children may have suffered, or may still be suffering fear, distress or emotional harm.

However, there can be a danger if we only emphasise the damage that domestic violence causes, without also pointing to the ways in which children can be supported to recover from these effects.

It can be useful therefore to talk about what might be protective factors in children's lives – things that can help children who have come through difficult experiences to remain emotionally healthy. Some of the most important protective factors for children are: having another caring adult in their life, having a safe haven they can go to, such as school, community group or sports team, and having good self-esteem.

So it is important to think of ways in which parents can enable rather than hinder these resilience factors in their children's lives. Unfortunately, while contact with other caring, non-abusive adults can be a powerful source of support for children, one of the effects of having violence in the home is that children can end up becoming isolated from the very people who could provide love, support and a view of the world that is not coloured by the abuse in the home.

Children who grow up with family violence may be directly told that they are not allowed to talk about what happens at home. However, children also seem to know without asking that they should keep what is going on a secret. This may be because they are afraid of what might happen if others found out, but also because children often feel very ashamed that their family is not 'normal'. They may hear or see violence and abuse, but discover that people around them never talk about it, and often behave as if it had never happened. As a result, children learn that this is a topic not to be talked about.

The following two exercises, adapted from an earlier manual written by Kate Iwi and Jo Todd (2000),[9] are designed to explore the effects of secrecy on children, to plan with parents ways they might enable their children to seek support and other influences in their lives, and to plan some simple appropriate ways of talking to children about violence they have experienced.

Exercise – The effects of secrecy

Aim

- To highlight the fact that hiding abuse can itself have very detrimental effects on children.

When violent parents make secrets of their violence, they usually make efforts to ensure that their partners and children keep quiet about it too. Victims of violence have their own reasons for secrecy as well.

First ask the parent you are working with to write down some of the reasons why he or she might hide their violence. Then go on to explore the following questions:

How do you think children might come to learn that they should keep the violence a secret?

Do your children talk to anyone about the violence? Who? Why might your children hide the violence by not talking about it?

What might be the negative effects of this secrecy on your children?

Are there realistic ways to diminish these negative effects?

If the parent you are working with grew up with a similar secret, the prompt questions below may also be helpful in guiding this discussion.

PICKING UP THE PIECES AFTER DOMESTIC VIOLENCE

If you were brought up in a family with a similar secret – maybe to do with violence, alcoholism, mental illness, sexual abuse or whatever – can you remember why you didn't tell?

What did it feel like to carry that secret, and how did it affect you?

What do you think would have helped you as a child?

What could you do to support your child to become less isolated without telling your child what to do?

Exercise – Talking to children about violence
Aims

- To work towards breaking the silence around family violence.

- To explore how to express accountability in a way appropriate to a child's age.

- To make parents aware that there are limits to what children will feel safe to discuss.

- To make a clear separation between explaining to children for the parents' sake and explaining for their sake.

Look at the developmental stages set out in Chapter 6. Ask the parent to suggest how violence in the family could be brought out into the open in a way that is appropriate to a child at each stage, using the following discussion points.

THE VIOLENCE

Should you mention it? Explain it? Apologise? If so, then how?

THE EFFECTS OF THE DOMESTIC VIOLENCE ON THE CHILD

Should you ask? Should you make guesses – if so, what are they?

Should you invite further discussion or permit your child to talk to others – if so, to whom?

THE CHILD'S OWN ANGER AND VIOLENCE

What might you say? How could you handle it if your child became violent?

When you discuss the parent's responses, use as a guide the question, 'How might that message or action help or harm your child?' There aren't right answers to these questions that apply to all children and all circumstances, so a thorough and specific and careful exploration in this way is the best way to proceed.

Note: If your considerations suggest that there could be benefits for a particular child of talking to them about the domestic violence, then go on to work towards developing a set of simple, age-appropriate messages that the parent could give about the violence (remembering that for those with more than one child, each will have had a different experience).

Talking to children about violence and abuse

Ask the parents what they have already said, if anything, to their children about the violence and abuse and what, if anything, the children have said.

If the parents witnessed or experienced abuse or violence as children, what would they have wanted the people who were abusive to say about it?

Help the parents to consider, child by child, what their children might need to hear about the abuse.

Try to keep them on track with the following suggestions:

- Use developmentally appropriate ideas and language.

- Always be open to listening to your children and/or discussing these issues when your children bring them up.

- Invite your children to ask or talk to you about these things and how they feel about them – say it might help to talk. Suggest they talk to other people about them and discuss who they might be able to go to. Reassure them that that's OK with you.

- If you want to bring up these issues, ask your children if it's OK to do so. If they show discomfort (even though they may say yes), then say 'Maybe you'd rather not or you feel too uncomfortable right now.' Give them a chance to verify whether or not this is so (e.g. 'I have done some things that were not right and that have hurt mummy and you. I would like to talk with you about this – is that OK?').

- Don't make promises you can't keep (e.g. 'I promise I'll never let him hurt me again' is unrealistic if you still live with the abuser) but do tell them what efforts you are making (e.g. 'I am really trying to change and not do this any more' or 'I am working at getting stronger so that I can keep us safe').

- Acknowledge without detail what happened (e.g. 'Daddy did some things that were wrong – he hit and hurt me.').

- If you were the victim, be clear the abuser was responsible without running him down to your children (e.g. 'There is no excuse for daddy hitting mummy or you. Violence is wrong, no matter how angry you get. No matter what you do, you don't deserve to be hit.'). If you were the abuser, be clear that what you did was your fault entirely.

- Reassure that not only was it not the children's fault but also that there wasn't anything they could have done about it either (e.g. 'It isn't even a bit your fault – you're too young/small to be able to control or stop an adult who is angry and not listening to you.').

- Be respectful and not blaming about the other parent, no matter how angry you feel.

- Tell them if you regret or feel sorry for what you did and for how it affected them (e.g. 'I am so sorry I hit mummy and even more sorry that I scared and upset you so much by doing it' or 'I am so sorry that you saw these things and that I didn't manage to protect you').

- Tell them that you love them while acknowledging you aren't perfect (e.g. 'I really love you even though I have hurt you/haven't managed to protect you from this. I can see how confusing that must be.').

- Give them a chance to speak out without pressuring them to do so (e.g. 'I am sure you have some very big feelings about this – maybe you feel angry or scared about it? Is there anything you want to tell me or ask me about it?').

- Permit them to talk to others about it (e.g. 'It would probably help to talk to someone about this – who do think you could talk to? I want you to know that's OK by me.').

Guard against parents rushing home to discuss their violence with children who may be terrified, or encouraging their children to talk about it with others unless the parents are ready to accept any possible come-back from that. Always put children's safety first. Some parents may want to take steps to alleviate effects on their children as quickly as possible. This is likely to be more about alleviating their own guilt, and may lead them to overlook the children's needs. Accountability to a child should be appropriate to the child's particular age, as well as based on the specific case in question. Even if a step seems safe and appropriate, advise that any discussions with children should be negotiated and agreed between both parents wherever that seems realistic and would be safe.

Parents' own childhoods

It can be difficult for some parents to benefit from the material we are presenting unless and until they can work a little at issues from their own childhoods.

All of us have internalised much more of our own parents' influence than we are ever consciously aware of. When we become parents, we may well find ourselves acting out parenting behaviours as if we had had beliefs or experiences that, on closer inspection, just aren't ours. A common example is the way that children of people who've lived with real food shortages often feed their own children as if they themselves felt that the supply may run out any day.

Equally, while any parent–child relationship will at times be emotionally intense, if we ourselves had distressing experiences during our childhood, the associated emotional charge can become re-activated in our interactions with our children. If this is the case, we may find ourselves feeling or reacting over-strongly.

If this is happening, it may be that the intensity of our reactions relates more to our own unresolved issues than to the behaviour of the child. If we want to be able to think clearly and parent our children in a loving and responsive way, it will be important to explore those issues to the extent that we can at least notice when our upset or anger with our child is out of proportion and take some simple steps to avoid overwhelming or frightening our child with our reactions.

There is much more extensive information on this topic in a book by Daniel Siegel and Mary Hartzell (2003) that provides both an accessible introduction to the scientific research on children's development and a range of exercises to help the reader explore how childhood experiences influence our parenting style.[10]

Ask a parent:

> Did you ever surprise yourself by doing or saying something to your child that you swore you would never do before you had children? How does that end up happening? (It might be useful for the worker to talk about an example from their own life if they have children).

It is inevitable that our parenting style will be influenced by our own experiences of being parented as a child. What's more, our early experiences of being parented take place at a time when we do not have the language or understanding of context to fully make sense of what is going on.

When we are children, because we don't start out with the ability to talk, and we don't have the understanding to make sense of what is happening around us, a lot of what we retain from our childhood are non-verbal memories, like the kind of memory that helps you tie your shoelace or drive a car – you don't consciously think of how to do it, you just find that you can remember how to do something even though you may not remember learning those skills or procedures.

As children, we learn ways of behaving by watching those around us – especially our parents – but these ways of behaving aren't consciously memorised: rather, they become little 'scripts' for action (we sometimes see children acting out these scripts in their make-believe games). As we get older, we may not realise we've held on to them until they are re-activated by similar situations when we ourselves become parents.

Reassessing what we've learned, and from where, can help us make some sense of our early lives, and it is the best way to help us avoid past experience shaping our parenting in ways we don't want.

The following exercise aims to open up these topics for discussion and to help parents to:

- begin to make the links between their own parenting style and their childhood experiences

- notice when emotional reactions linked to past experience may lead them to behave in ways they don't want to

- take steps to avoid this – simple calming exercises and positive self-talk are good first steps.

This is an area where complex and painful issues may come up, which may not be resolvable in the time you have to work with parents. If it becomes apparent that parents you are working with suffered repeated and severe trauma as children, it may be that you will want to recommend that they speak with a counsellor or therapist who has experience in this area, or who can provide longer-term help to recover from and make sense of these experiences.

✎ Exercise – Own parents
Aims

- To help parents:

  ◦ reflect on their own experience of being parented

  ◦ become more aware of where and how they learned their own parenting behaviours

  ◦ become better able to consciously choose their parenting behaviours.

This is a deceptively simple exercise. Our experience is that these few questions can form the basis for a rich and sometimes emotional discussion about parents' childhood experiences, both positive and negative. Be aware that some parents will have painful memories of their childhoods; others will have an idealised view of one or both parents, and will struggle with a sense of disloyalty at being asked to name parenting behaviours they did not like. Allow plenty of time to talk through the issues that arise and to reflect on how past experience has shaped their hopes for their own children.

Suggested discussion questions

- What really irritates you about your child?

- Which child do you find harder to manage?

- What feelings come up when things are most difficult?

- What thoughts do you notice going through your head when things are hardest with this child?

- How are you seeing your child at this point?

- Describe your main carers or parents with three words for each of them.

- Which one were you closer to?

- Why were you less close to the other parent or carer?

- In what ways are you least like them?

- How did they handle their anger?

- In what form (if any) did they allow your anger?

- In what form (if any) did they allow your neediness?

- How does this relate to what you said earlier about the things you find hardest to manage and tolerate in your own children?

- How did your own parents discipline you?

- How did you react?

- How did they express love and affection?

- How did they praise you?

- How did they put you down or criticise you?

- In what ways are you similar to your parents in the way you treat your children?

- What do you appreciate about the way you were parented? Tell me about some of the things you got from each of your parents that you would like to repeat in your own parenting.

- What do you resent about the way you were parented? Tell me about some of the ways you want to parent your own children differently.

- What can you tell yourself when your own childhood issues come up in your relationship with your child? Examples might be 'I'm really angry but it's not all about him'; 'I'm the grown-up here, I need to be bigger, wiser and kind'; 'This is my stuff.'

- How has it been to talk about these things? What have you been realising as we've had this discussion?

- What can you learn from coming up against these issues again? How might this help you grow as a person and a parent?

6 Helping Parents Understand Their Children's Development

An essential part of child-centred parenting is being able to adapt to our children's changing needs and capabilities as they grow. So it is important to provide parents with a reasonable and accurate view of what is age appropriate, normal, and excusable child behaviour (it may also be useful to focus on specific problems and abilities of children with developmental difficulties).

As workers, it is also important to be aware that abusive parenting is more likely in parents who are habitually critical and blaming of their children. This is usually accompanied by unrealistic expectations of children's capabilities or inappropriate attributions about their motives ('She's doing it on purpose'; 'He's trying to ruin my day'; 'He's sly, he's lazy, he's deliberately defying me'). We can help parents be more empathetic and understanding by enabling them to learn more about what is realistic to expect of children.

The material that follows is designed to be used as handouts to give to parents. As you talk through the handouts, try to find out what resonates with parents – what is recognisable? As far as possible, ask the parents for stories and examples relating to their own children. It may be helpful to choose one child and reflect together on how much the information here applies to that child.

Educational input on developmental stages

Work through the handouts that apply to the ages of the parents' children. Before doing so, explain that:

- Children develop through a series of stages – they may progress slowly or quickly but they don't skip any stages altogether.

- Just because a child's behaviour doesn't fall into the age range associated with the developmental stage, the child's behaviour may still be considered 'normal'.

- There is a spiralling progression with occasional steep upward steps. Mostly, children move gradually from one stage to the next, initially showing more behaviour from the lower level stage and eventually showing more from the higher level stage.

- Lower levels are rarely left behind altogether. People often speak of 'our inner child' – the scared or angry or abandoned toddler who sometimes runs the show in adulthood unless well taken care of.

- It is also evident that we all regress under stress to a time when our needs were better met: adults do when ill, toddlers do when another baby is born and trauma often leads to regressive behaviours.

- 'Understanding' precedes 'thinking' and 'doing'. Children will understand higher stage reasoning in discussion with adults but will 'think' at a lower stage when making decisions on their own.

- Development may stop at any stage. This might be because children have reached their mental or physical limits, because of trauma or because there are emotional obstacles or preoccupations preventing further development.

Developmental stage – Baby development 0–2

Omnipotent – 'Limit? What's a limit?'

- Your child is developing movement and coordination.

- Your child is mostly developmentally unable to respond to commands.

- The brain is still developing and the areas most used will end up more developed.

- Your child is watching and starting to interact (crying, first smile at about 2–3 months, etc.). The rapport you establish will give the child a template for future close relationships (often called an 'attachment style').

- It is easy to expect too much of your 1–2-year-old – despite their mobility, toddlers may totally lack a sense of danger or fear.

- Do not expect a toddler to share toys, wait for food in a restaurant, or be patient while you try on clothes or go food shopping.

- Aggressive behaviours – hitting and biting – are common at this age. How parents respond to this behaviour determines if it will continue.

- Some children show readiness for toilet training between 18 and 24 months, but most don't.

Parenting

- Always check when your baby seems uncomfortable, to make sure the infant is not too hot, too cold, hungry, wet or needs to burp, and do not worry about 'spoiling' at this age.

- Parents cannot always console their baby. Expect this.

- Hold, cuddle, talk to, sing to and rock your baby as much as you can. A lot of development depends on your infant's interaction with you. Play face to face with your baby, who will begin to develop a sense of trust and the beginning elements of learning through games like peekaboo. While positive interaction stimulates a baby's normal brain development, scary or neglectful parenting can stimulate the stress response functions to over-develop leading to an exaggerated flight-fright-freeze response.

- Encourage 'speaking' by talking to your baby lots.

- Stimulate interest with age-appropriate toys so that your infant can begin watching and reaching. Babies like to bounce, swing, reach for you, pick up and drop objects, and bang things together.

- Provide opportunities for safe exploration.

- Make sure you get adequate rest. Encourage dad and other family members to help care for your infant. Keep in contact with friends and relatives.

Discipline

- From around 6 months, parents can begin to set some groundwork for future discipline by using distraction, reducing stimulation and establishing routines – for example, a bedtime routine.

- By 9 months, you can begin to set limits by using verbal 'no's', distraction, removing the object from the baby's sight or removing the baby from the object.

- Consistency of discipline is very important.

- Don't expect the infant to follow your commands – let alone to stick to your limits. Don't get angry with your baby for not doing so. You are only introducing the idea of a limit at this stage.

- Praise the child for good behaviour.

- Temper tantrums are best handled by keeping children safe (some parents firmly and gently hold their child from behind) but ignoring them. If this is not possible, isolate the child in a safe playpen or room for a 'time-out'. Never use shouting or spanking.

- Keep rules to a minimum. Long speeches of explanation are completely useless. 'Because I said so!' should be enough.

- When disciplining, try to make a verbal separation between the child and his or her behaviour ('I love you, but I do not like it when you touch the TV').

- Provide alternatives: 'No, you cannot play with the telephone, but you can play with these blocks.'

- Avoid power struggles with your toddler. No one wins!

- Don't start toilet training before a child is ready. This will only cause the child to rebel and the child could still be in nappies at 3 and 4 years of age. It is important not to shame a child during toilet training.

Developmental stage – Pre-school development 2–4

Egocentric – 'I should do/get what I want'
Testing boundaries

- Your 2–4-year-old is finding and testing boundaries and will often attempt to assert independence.

- 2–4-year-olds are self-centred (egocentric) and think that what they want is right. They will say that it's 'not fair' whenever they don't get their own way.

- Thinking is concrete (your child can't generalise between varying situations or hold rules in mind consistently).

- Children of this age group take what you say literally.

- A 2-year-old is difficult, if not impossible, to reason with. As your child turns 3 and 4, you may find that this shifts a little.

- Your 2–4-year-old will understand the command when you give it, but be unable to stop breaking the rule when you're not around.

- The 3–4-year-old will ask lots of questions.

- Your child may well lie when caught – often blatantly and badly and without realising this is wrong.

- Modesty and a desire for privacy begin to emerge as young as 4 years old.

- Encourage, but do not expect, sharing at 2 years old – by 3, children will sometimes begin to take turns and share but mostly need prompting to do so. The default is for them to think in terms of 'It's mine', 'I want it'.

- By 3 years, playmates are important. Allow your child to experience interaction with peers.

- A toddler's appetite is rarely what most parents think it should be. Children can be 'faddy' and fussy with their choices. Feeding problems may arise if you make your children eat more than they need to, or show too much concern about what they eat.

Discipline and parenting

- Parents must teach their children that there are rules they must follow – you should show your child where the boundaries are.

- Rules need to be concrete, specific and consistent.

- Do not waste time and breath arguing or reasoning. 'Because I said so!' should still be enough at 2 years, but as children get towards 3 and 4 years old more explanations will be needed. They will be able to understand a higher level of reasoning than the level they can apply on their own.

- Environmental controls should be used a lot.

- Lying should be discussed but not punished.

- Continue to praise your child for good behaviour.

- Don't use sarcasm or make extreme threats to your child (e.g. 'If you carry on like that, you're going into an orphanage') – at this age they may take what you say very literally.

- Meaningless threats are ineffective. Follow through with the previously stated consequences when rules are broken.

- When your child starts to want privacy, make it clear that you think this is good.

- Whenever possible, give reprimands privately – especially with 4-year-olds upwards.

- Maintain a consistent bathtime and bedtime routine. Using a night light, security blanket or toy are all ways to help lessen night-time fears, which are common at this stage.

- Encourage your 2–4-year-old to make choices whenever possible, but the choices should be limited to those you can live with ('red shirt or green shirt'). Never ask a 2-year-old an open question ('Do you want to take a bath?') unless you are willing to accept the answer.

- Provide alternatives. If your 2-year-old is playing with something unacceptable, replace it with another object or toy that your child enjoys. 'No, you cannot play with the telephone, but you can play with these blocks.' This avoids a fight.

- Avoid power struggles. Two-year-olds use the temper tantrum when angry, tired, frustrated or not getting their way. Safely contain and ignore the tantrums.

- Pick your battles. Don't make toilet training or eating your battle grounds. Decide on a few rules – most of which have to do with the child's safety – and enforce them.

Toilet training

- Your children will learn to control their urine and bowel movements when they are developmentally ready, just as they learned to sit, walk and talk. It takes an inordinate effort to speed up a child's schedule compared to 'catching that developmental wave' and teaching when the child is ready. In fact, by over-training, you may delay the process by making your child tense and nervous, resulting in a rebellion. The last thing parents want to do is to make toilet training become a battle ground, which could possibly lay the groundwork for a real 'toilet problem' in years to come. By age 4, 95 per cent of children are bowel trained, 90 per cent of children are dry in the daytime and 75 per cent are dry at night.

- Signs of toilet-learning readiness include awakening from a nap dry, having bowel movements at the same time each day, being able to say 'wee-wee' or 'poo-poo', etc., knowing when they have to go, and being able to take off their own clothes.

- If your children have bowel movements at the same time every day, you can sit them on a potty and 'catch it'. A favourable response sends a positive message to a child. If on the other hand, your child's bowel movements occur at irregular times during the day, watch for a characteristic expression and posture that indicates a bowel movement. When this occurs, pick the child up and put them on the potty. If nothing happens in a few minutes, or if the child is are alarmed in any way, take them off the potty.

- Your child's incentive to control bladder and bowel movements is to please you so praise your child's accomplishments. When your child has an 'accident,' stay calm and don't punish. If you act distressed or angry when the child fails, training may be delayed.

Developmental stage – Infant development 5–6

Obedient – 'I should do what I'm told'

- Children are now more cooperative and focused on what authority figures tell them is right – although they still aren't able to figure out the principles underlying the rules and tend to be morally simplistic (very 'black and white' about moral issues).

- The 5–6-year-old's rule following is out of obedience to authority and so it is very difficult to teach children this age about personal safety issues that involve protecting themselves from potentially abusive adults.

- Children follow rules so as not to get into trouble and because they want to please authority figures.

- Your 5–6-year-old may imagine that adults are all-knowing and can always catch children when they're bad.

- Children may tell tales excessively because they see adults as the only source of authority.

- Children at this age tend to believe that, if something bad happens to them, they must have done something bad to deserve it.

Discipline and parenting

- Parents have to teach the reasons underlying the rules without expecting children to fully grasp these yet. Asking children to explain why they think certain courses of action are right might help them to develop their reasoning – but don't expect sophisticated answers yet.

- Use praise and praise systems such as star charts, which need not lead to more concrete rewards, to teach and modify your child's behaviour. At this age these kinds of methods are very effective and also help build self-esteem.

- Avoid physical punishment – it only promotes fear and guilt and teaches the child that violence is acceptable in certain situations.

- Recognise that a child's sexual curiosity and exploration are normal.

- You can role play danger situations with your child giving as many concrete examples as possible. Don't stress stranger-danger over danger from your friend, the parents of your child's friends, family and older children.

- Children should learn that genitals are private (not bad or shameful – just private). You can suggest that your children never go off with anyone, touch anyone or allow anyone to touch their genitals without asking you first. This way they can combat one authority figure with a rule from another.

- It is not unusual for a 6-year-old to have occasional toileting accidents at night and during play. Be understanding and do not make a big deal out of it. However, if it happens frequently, do discuss the matter with the child's doctor.

- Adults play important roles in the life of children at age 6. Children will develop close relationships with teachers. It can be really helpful for your child to discuss things that make them sad, angry or anxious with their teachers. Actively let your children know that they can talk to their teacher or other family members about your family's problems – even if you feel embarrassed for others to know about these.

Developmental stage – Junior development 7–11

Pre-adolescent – Consequence-focused – 'What's in it for me?'
Comparing – 'If she can do it, why can't I?'

- Children are still focused on what adults think is right, but now also on the consequences of their choices and on concrete rewards.

- The growing influence of peers often presents a challenge to parents. Children aged 7–11 are beginning to value their peers' opinions as well as their parents'. But, at this age, parent opinion and values are still the strongest.

- The 7–11-year-old increasingly believes that everything should be equal. This can lead to a lot of fighting and arguing among peer groups.

- Children's increasing belief that things should be equal may lead them to make constant comparisons, to want what they perceive their friends to have and to challenge parents when they don't live by their own rules.

- Relationships are seen as 'deals' – 'You play with me because I played with you.'

- On the other hand, while their choices may be based on this kind of deal making, their thinking is becoming increasingly abstract so that they begin to be able to learn values and to apply moral judgements to new situations.

- The 7–11-year-old is starting to think much more about what goes on for others – they can now 'empathise'.

- They are also more skilled at using lying and cheating to get their way.

- The 7–11-year-old can appear very mature at some moments and very childish at others. They still often don't think about consequences for themselves and others when in the midst of making choices and decisions.

Discipline and parenting

- Parents have to teach their children natural consequences and empathy – children have to learn how their behaviour has an impact on themselves and on others.

- Concrete reward and consequence systems work particularly well at this age.

- You can appeal to your child's 'tit-for-tat' thinking – 'I did this for you, now you do this for me' or 'If you want privileges, show some responsibility'.

- Meanwhile teach more abstract values and constructive ways to deal with conflict.

- Parents have to continue to use praise a lot and to listen. Children who feel good about themselves are better equipped to withstand negative peer pressure.

- Provide personal space for your children at home, even if it's limited, and meet their increasing needs for bodily privacy.

- Find good friends for your child. Promote interaction and allegiance with peers through participation in social activities, community groups and team sports.

- Help your children learn how to get along with their peers. Talk to them about the enjoyable and difficult aspects of friendships.

- While you should establish fair rules with respect to TV watching, outside activities, homework, bedtime, etc., the number of rules should be kept to a minimum. As the role of peers in the life of a 7–11-year-old builds, so they may increasingly resist adult authority.

- Understand the importance of acting as a parental role model. Your children will now feel less afraid of challenging your opinions and behaviour and will expect you to follow the rules you set them (it's part of their desire for equality).

- Encourage age-appropriate independence and self-responsibility.

- Do not wait until your children are mature to talk to them about some of the changes taking place in their classmates. You are wrong if you think a 10-year-old is still too young to talk about such things. Prepare your daughter for menstruation. Prepare your son for wet dreams. Begin to teach your children about pregnancy and sexually transmitted diseases, including AIDS.

Developmental stage – Early adolescent development 12–16

Conformity – 'What will my mates think?'
Separation – pushing the boundaries again

- Your early adolescent will bounce between childhood and adulthood, being irresponsible and responsible, testing parental authority and then depending on it.

- Dramatic physical changes are the hallmark of early adolescence and these physical changes are important to adolescents. They signify that they are developing like their peers. Because many young adolescents are unaware that the onset and rate of puberty vary greatly, they need reassurance that their own growth and development are normal. Moreover, many children this age need 9–10 hours of sleep per night.

- They feel insecure about themselves, critical of others and in great need of peer approval.

- Many young adolescents, preoccupied with their attractiveness, will try to change their appearance through dieting or consumer fad food products. Anorexia and bulimia may occur especially among females.

- Children aged 11–16 can now judge behaviour more deeply – not just 'Does it fit the rules?' and 'Who does it benefit?', but also asking themselves 'Were the motives good?'

- Even so, adolescents are now focused on what their peers think is right and on the consequences for themselves – these will tend to determine the choices that they make.

- In their early teens children often challenge adult authority – the subtle moral thinking might well be applied to your behaviour more than to their own.

- Teenagers are gaining a sense of their own maleness or femaleness. Curiosity about sexual matters begins. They begin having sexual feelings centred around their own bodies, rather than developing sexual relationships with the opposite sex. Accurate information needs to be made available and you may need to think about the extent of your own comfort or discomfort in discussing these matters.

- With their increasing mobility and independence, there is potential for exploration of risky behaviours. Substance use and sexual activity increase with each successive year of secondary school.

Discipline and parenting

- Parents should teach their early adolescents to think for themselves and make good choices, to problem solve, and to think about how to achieve their own goals.

- Special athletic, artistic, academic or musical talents may emerge and should be encouraged and supported as much as possible. This will help your adolescent to develop a good self-image.

- Try to encourage reasonable independence, friendships and interests outside the home, at times stepping aside a little in favour of mentor relationships.

- Get to know your children's friends, and avoid making quick judgements based on appearances only. Whenever possible, avoid criticising their friends and encourage them to invite peers home.

- Use family rule meetings and give increasing responsibility to your adolescent for setting family rules and enforcing them.

- Involve your teenagers in decision making regarding their role in family chores, supervision of younger siblings, etc. Once chores around the home are agreed, provide an allowance.

- Take pleasure in your son's or daughter's abilities and achievements.

- Respect your adolescent's privacy.

- Do not criticise the other parent. A teenager needs to love and respect both parents.

- Pick your battles – minimise criticism, nagging, derogatory comments and other belittling or demeaning messages.

- Show respect. Listens to your adolescent's side of the story without interrupting or judging.

- Your adolescents will benefit from learning about body changes during puberty, including variations from individual to individual. They also need to learn about birth control and sexually transmitted diseases as well as ways to say no to sex.

- Be honest. Teens ask difficult questions that may need complex answers. It may be hard for us to know exactly how to formulate answers, so tell them what you are experiencing. Allow them to understand how you are formulating the answers. This is a great way to encourage thinking through their own decisions, and helping them learn to decrease their impulsiveness.

- Use humour.

- Check with them how things are going. Ask questions, but don't expect answers.

- Understand that their moods will change quickly and without warning. Try to stay with them and follow their lead.

- Feelings of sadness and depression should not be dismissed as 'normal' moodiness during this period. Situational losses – including the death of a pet, problems with girlfriends or boyfriends, school failure and parental disappointment – can lead to depression and even suicide. Learn the signs of adolescent depression and drug abuse.

- Discuss with your adolescent how to resist peer pressure and not just 'go' with the crowd. Role play how to say no to drugs and make possible contingency plans in the event that a car trip is necessary and the adolescent (or the person who is driving) is drunk or has taken drugs.

- Don't believe that how your adolescent behaves is somehow a reflection on you.

- Take joy in your children's creativity and express empathy for them in their struggle. Try to remember how you felt as a teenager, and consider what may have helped you through these trials and tribulations.

- Be available to your adolescents without directing or controlling them. The time when they will want you is often at their choosing, not yours. Be there if possible.

- At toddler stage when you and your child had battles for control, you ultimately had to win. At adolescence the battles are on again, only this time your task is to begin to lose – to let go of control with grace – starting with the less important battles. Say 'yes' when you can but 'no' when you must.

Developmental stage – Young adult development 17–19

Principle-focused – 'Respect all people's rights'

- Older teens/young adults have a strong abstract sense of right and wrong – often 'in principle' with little allowance for practicalities and context. They begin to think about society in a very theoretical way, stepping back from their own society and considering the rights and values that a society ought to uphold. They then evaluate existing societies in terms of these prior considerations. Idealism is often at a height and their commitment to justice makes the rationale for civil disobedience stronger and broader.

- At the age of 18, adolescents begin to recognise that parents can be their best friends.

- The peer group becomes less important to the late adolescent and is replaced by a few good friends. The young adult's interests now focuses on education or a vocational future.

- Older adolescents are more independent of peer pressure and have internalised values, empathy and conscience.

Discipline and parenting

- The role of parents during this phase in their children's development should be one of support. Parents will usually find that their children have a better relationship with them now than they did in the early teen years. The adolescent may even seek out their advice.

- Involve them in decisions and discussions about the family – ask their opinions and advice.

- Encourage them to speak their minds and listen to them.

- Encourage them to listen to and try to understand others' decisions and opinions alongside their own.

- Most young people have opportunities to experiment with drugs and alcohol by this stage, and parents have little power to prevent such opportunities from arising. A major objective should be to get adolescents through this stage alive and intact. Parents should be frank and realistic about the dangers of substance use and of mixing drinking and/or drugs with driving. Young people know too much about these issues for scaremongering to work. You can offer to provide transportation – no questions asked – rather than have them take a lift with a driver who has been drinking or using drugs.

7 Child to Parent Violence and Out-of-control Behaviour – Becoming More Parent-centred

Child to parent violence is often kept hidden within families, but is nonetheless quite common. While the majority of very young children hit their parents at some time or other, violence by older children and teenagers can become distressing and frightening. Large-scale surveys haven't yet been carried out in the UK, but studies carried out in the USA indicate that violence to parents by older children occurs in about 10 per cent of families there, and perhaps unsurprisingly the severity of such violence increases with the age of the child.[11]

What factors contribute to this phenomenon? Children who have witnessed domestic violence are much more likely to be violent to their parents, as are children who have lived with coercive parenting or physical punishment – especially if this was serious and persistent. These factors are also linked with increased likelihood of violence in future adult relationships, which highlights the importance of helping children to recover from the effects of exposure to violence.

However, child to parent violence can also happen in families where violence has not been present. Indeed in Australia, Eddie Gallagher has found that in about half of the families he works with there is no evidence of previous violence. These tend to be two-parent families, often educated and middle class, where parents have an 'over-indulgent' parenting style and find it difficult to set limits for their children. In these families children may grow up with such a strong sense of entitlement that they start to bully a parent or parents to get their own way.[12]

However, in families where there has been domestic violence, the issues are different; here it seems to be more about guilty disempowered parents and traumatised angry teenagers battling it out. Most single parents who have been victims of domestic violence are women and this chapter is written primarily with them in mind. However, there may be fathers who have been victims of domestic violence for whom this work is equally useful, or couples/blended families who are living together after the domestic violence has stopped and who may equally find themselves facing out-of-control children and teens.

It is important to note that a lot of violence from children to parents can't be considered abusive at all, and so the exercises outlined in this chapter would not be applicable to, for example:

- play getting out of hand

- violence by very young children

- children or young people suffering psychosis (however, the work in this chapter would be applicable to children with ADHD or oppositional defiant disorder [ODD])

- children fighting back to a parent who has abused them

- attempts to defend one parent from violence by the other.

While much of the work presented here would be useful for any parents who are being victimised by their children, we will focus on interventions for parents whose parenting and coping strategies have been undermined by past abuse. While you can work on child behaviour management techniques with such a parent, if their ability to set and protect their boundaries is damaged, if they feel terrified of their child, or if they are feeling excessively guilty or ashamed, then they simply won't be able to use them.

The dynamics of child to parent violence

A mother who has experienced domestic violence is likely to have been disempowered within her family. In some cases, she may have entered her relationship with considerable personal vulnerabilities that will have contributed to her difficulties in setting clear boundaries and prioritising her own safety and well-being. However, any parent is likely to end up feeling guilty, disempowered or depressed if they have experienced ongoing domestic violence. Children who have lived with the abuse of a parent can all too easily end up being controlling and violent to that parent themselves and getting away with it – and this can start at a surprisingly young age.

Children may be angry about what they have been through – indeed they may even be living life in a constant state of resentment – and the impacts of trauma may have left them with a reduced stimulus-response threshold. In this state, seemingly small irritants can lead to their 'blowing their top'. Additionally, they may be angry with the victimised parent for failing to protect herself and them, or they may have adopted the abuser's world view and genuinely blame the victim for 'provoking' the abuse. These are children who have learned that violence is synonymous with anger and that it can be used to get your own way. They have learned to see frightening behaviour as 'normal' and they've learned to see one parent (usually their mum) as deserving of abuse. What's more, although some children fight back against an abusive parent when they reach their teenage years, for most the prospect is always going to remain too scary. The victim – usually the mum – is a safer target (although younger siblings can also be on the receiving end). The relationship between mother and child does not necessarily improve after the abusive partner leaves and the violence that has ruled the family stops. In some families children may start to 'act out' because they feel safe to do so. However, because they have been used to fear-based discipline, and the mother's authority has been damaged in their eyes, the children may be relatively immune to her attempts to set boundaries – particularly because she is unlikely to be able to (or want to) match the level of power that has been exerted in the past. In this situation, children may start to misuse their growing personal and physical power themselves. With older teenagers that can mean their using violence and abuse towards the parent they live with.

What's the best approach to take?

It stands to reason that, if the key problems in such a person's parenting style are their sense of undeservedness, difficulty in setting meaningful boundaries, fear and guilt, then interventions are needed that:

- decrease guilt
- increase parents' sense of worth and entitlement
- encourage clear boundary setting
- manage fear through safety planning
- provide behaviour management techniques that can be put in place even when the power relationship is still 'upside down'.

Essentially this area of parenting work can borrow much from the work to help victims of domestic violence more generally – diminishing self-blame, naming what is abusive and unacceptable, encouraging parents to see themselves as the solution but not the problem, safety planning and identifying what supports are available to the parent.

Guilt

In the introduction to this book we considered the effects of domestic violence on children and on parenting. It's easy for this sort of information to leave a parent, who is already prone to self-blame, feeling really guilty even though they were the victim, not the perpetrator of the domestic violence. This kind of undeserved 'victim-shame' is terribly unfair but it is probably in part motivated by a psychological need to believe that the world is a safe and fair place to live in. Because we hate to believe that bad things can happen to anybody, we tend to think that a victim of an assault must have done something concrete to deserve it. In this way we create a false sense of safety and justice and control over our situation. If we can just avoid doing that particular thing or action, then we will not come to harm. In the same way, victims of violence tend to believe that, if they could just have acted differently, the violence would not have happened. It may also feel easier to blame yourself rather than believe that someone you loved has deliberately hurt you.

So parents already feel guilty towards their children, and then, to compound it all, feel doubly ashamed when they are unable to control them.

The point to make to parents is that there is no such thing as a perfect parent – ideas about good parenting change radically from decade to decade and culture to culture, and the variations are more down to changing trends than scientific breakthroughs or different 'knowledge'.

The kind of parenting that fosters a 'laid-back' attitude in a child won't also foster drive; the kind that fosters independence won't also encourage the ability to show vulnerabilities. Similarly, a parenting style that works well with one child might not work so well with another.

Children need to learn that things can go wrong, people make mistakes, and that healing and repair are possible. This is as important a life lesson as any. But it doesn't mean that anything goes parenting-wise and that there's a totally open playing field – instead there is a zone of 'good enough' parenting in which a parent is able to meet a child's needs.

In a normal situation with an average child, you can be a 'good enough' parent so long as you aren't frequently or severely abusive, are fairly involved, and are neither wholly indulgent and permissive nor wholly authoritarian. However, the 'isolated-single-parent-family-post-domestic-violence-with-out-of-control-children' is still a relatively new phenomenon – so, despite the fact that such families are increasingly prevalent, there isn't much in terms of a prevailing trend about how a good enough parent *should* be. It's a very difficult situation. The parent may well be doing a good enough job already for a normal circumstance, but she may be struggling in a situation where to be a good enough parent requires almost super-human qualities of firmness, understanding, consistency, bravery and patience (to name but a few).

Exercise – Is it all my fault?

This exercise has been adapted from Eddie Gallagher's 'Who's in Charge?' programme. It has been designed to help parents to get some perspective on just how much of a causal influence they have had on their children's out-of-control behaviour. The point of this is to diminish their self-blame and guilt.

A parent is encouraged to think of one child at a time and to fill out the worksheet, 'Is it all my fault?'.

Is it all my fault?

This activity is about how much influence you have had on your child's out-of-control behaviour. It focuses on just one child and only on what has influenced that child acting in that way.

> How old is this child?
>
> Boy or girl?
>
> Are you the mother or father?

Think of *your* causal influence on this child's out-of-control behaviour as amounting to 10 points. Compared with your 10 points of influence, how much causal influence do you think the other parent has had on the same scale? If the other parent has half as much influence as you, award 5 points, if twice your influence, give 20 points, etc. It might be that schoolfriends have had 50 points of influence – 5 times as many as you – on your child's out-of-control behaviour. Go as high as necessary. You can award 0 points for things that were irrelevant to the development of these behaviours. Equally, you can give people points even if they weren't around in your child's life if you think that they have had an influence by their absence.

This is not an exact science – give the scores that first come into your mind rather than labouring over them to try and achieve accuracy.

Points

- Your influence

- The other parent

- Relationship between parents

- Step-parents

- Brothers and sisters

- Other relatives

- School

- Friends

- Any other people

- TV, other media

- Temperament (elements of personality your child was born with) ☐
- Physical (appearance, size, health, age reaching puberty) ☐
- Free will and child's own choices ☐
- Specific events ☐
- Any other influences ☐

When you've finished, compare how much influence you have had alongside all the other influences in your child's life.

Note: If you've got a calculator, you can work out what percentage of the total influence on your child is your contribution. Divide your number of points (10) by the total number of squares filled in, and multiply by 100 to give a rough indication of your percentage influence on the out-of control behaviour.

Points to note

- This is not a scientific or accurate measure, just a rough indicator. It probably underestimates the importance of parents…but not by very much unless a parent is unusually bad! Sadly it is far easier to be a bad influence than a good one.

- This is definitely *not* a measure of good or bad parenting. There are no good or bad scores. If it seems that you don't have a lot of influence, this may mean that your child lives an active, interesting life or has a strong personality, not that you are unimportant. A high score may mean that you have a younger child, that you are very close and important to each other, or it could mean that your child has few other contacts and is isolated.

- Parents are like air or water. They are *essential* even if other influences appear to be greater. Because you are *one of* the biggest influences on your child, you still have a huge responsibility to do your best and even small influences can make a profound difference at the right time.

- However, is it realistic for you to either take full responsibility for your child's achievements or (more commonly) to take all the blame for your child's problems? Guilt gets in the way of parents being firm and assertive with children, and often causes unnecessary stress or grief.

- We need to be realistic about what we can and can't control and what we can and can't influence. But paradoxically, our taking too much responsibility for causing our children's behaviour may mean their taking less responsibility for changing it.

✎ Exercise – Exploring guilt and shame

It can really help to get the shame and self-blame out on the table, and a good way to do this without reinforcing these attitudes still further is to ask your client (usually a mother) to 'externalise' her shaming/self-blaming/guilty self-talk in order to get some distance from which to explore it more. This technique, from narrative therapy, may seem a bit odd at first, so do practise it a bit until you get a feel for it. If you want to read more about it then have a look at the work of Michael White (2009) who developed these approaches, or you can try the introductory text by Alice Morgan (2000).[13,14]

The trick with this technique is to keep talking about and thinking of shame or the idea of being a 'bad parent' as a thing existing outside of the person. By far the easiest way to do that is to get the client to draw, collage or represent this on paper so that it can be pointed to.

Start by characterising it – putting it out on the table:

Can we look more at this 'shame/self-blame/guilt/ bad parent' thing?

Would you call it that or what should we call it?

If it was a character, what would it look like?

Describe its energy and posture – imagine it on that chair – how does it sit?

How does it feel to have it around?

Then look at its operation in early life:

When did (shame) first appear in your life?

What was going on that brought it into your life?

What things did it tell you to convince you to let it in?

What purpose did it serve for you early on?

Explore how it operates nowadays:

How does it affect you and your life now?

Is it a friend or foe?

What does it whisper in your ear?

Has it borrowed the voice of anyone from your past?

What does it say to you about your parenting?

How does it affect your ability to be a strong parent?

What things does it convince you to do or not do?

What things does it convince you to allow or put up with?

How does it do that?

Look at the control your client has over it:

> How do you frustrate or sabotage it when it's up to its tricks?

> What strengths have you got that help you send it away when you don't want it around?

> What do you tell yourself when you want to send it away?

Allow ambivalent mixed feelings towards the thing being externalised:

> What have you learned from it that can be useful in your life?

> It you could send it packing, what would you miss most about it?

> Would you want to keep it some times and not others?

And finally, review and wrap up the conversation:

> What's it been like to look at this (shame) thing the way we've been doing?

> What have you realised?

> What steps might this conversation lead you to take in the future?

> What shall we do with the picture or collage you've drawn? We could put 'put it away' somewhere, knowing that it's there though and knowing that it will still come out sometimes. I can put it in your file here, or we can we bin it or even ceremonially shred it?

Control

✎ Exercise – Why does my teenager abuse me?
Aims

- To bring attention to the controlling aspects of child–parent abuse.

- To help parents identify how they can change what happens in the home after a child is violent, so that there isn't an inadvertent payoff for the abuse.

Many parents assume that, because their child has grown up with domestic violence (and also sometimes has a diagnosis of ADHD or ODD, etc.), this is the reason the child is violent. While undoubtedly these are important factors in learning to be violent and in finding it hard to use more emotionally regulated ways of dealing with conflict, they do not mean that the young person has to be violent. Unless the teenager is severely disabled or psychotic, then there is still a choice as to whether to use violence, and a controlling intention.

Ask the parents to generate three story scenarios in which their children typically abuse them. Ask them to say what sparked the argument off and how the argument developed. For each scenario:

1. Tell the parents that people abuse to try to control the way another person acts. Ask how the abusing teenager in each of their scenarios wanted the

parent to act differently. Ask why the teenager might have wanted them to act differently.

It's important to identify whether there is a payoff for the children in behaving in a violent or hurtful way, and, if so, what it is. If being violent, or shouting and swearing, has in the past meant that the children are more likely to get their own way, or that people are less likely to make demands upon them, then the behaviour has a payoff. This is true whether or not the children are consciously aware of this (however, many young people report being quite aware that aggression helps them get their own way). It's a lot easier to stick with the difficult task of setting consequences for bad behaviour if you understand this. If you see your child's behaviour as a symptom of your failures as a parent or as being caused by a psychological disorder, you are more likely to feel guilty and helpless and less likely to be able to act assertively.

2. Tell the parents that people abuse to change the way they feel in the moment. Ask how the teenagers in their scenarios wanted to feel differently by using abuse and what feelings they were trying to avoid – what feelings would they have been left with if they hadn't been abusive?

Being violent may make children feel more powerful and more in control. If they are feeling unhappy and angry, they may want to make their parents feel as bad as they do, because at that age children feel that their parents are responsible for everything. Some parents may be acutely aware of their children's hurt and vulnerability, but again it's important that we don't give children unintended payoffs for being abusive. It is also still important to set clear boundaries about how it's OK to behave when you feel bad. Otherwise children will learn the lesson that it is acceptable to frighten or hurt people if you feel hurt yourself – which will have damaging consequences for all their relationships.

Parents might think about how they can 'speak to' and comfort the hurt feelings without giving in. For example, saying 'I know it's really horrible when you can't buy what you want and that not having the money leaves you feeling out of control and low. I feel like that myself when I want things and just can't get them.' Consequences and boundaries can stay in place alongside empathy. At first these ways of talking might bounce right off young people's defences but ultimately this is a way to gradually teach them to be able to think about and tolerate more vulnerable emotions – a very important part of growing up.

Putting clear boundaries in place

In Chapter 4 we outlined steps for child-centred behaviour management (to recap, these were: modelling the behaviour you want to encourage; giving praise and attention for good behaviour; being able to ignore some bad behaviour; giving clear, firm instructions; rewarding behaviour you want to encourage and implementing consequences). Re-establishing safety and righting the power structure in a home where a child is victimising a parent will involve the same steps. However, because of the physical risks, extra care will need to be taken when planning to implement these steps, and the parents will need extra support if they are to implement and sustain change in the face of distressing and frightening behaviour from their children.

What seems to be most important here is a change in parental attitude, the very fact that the parent is 'stepping up' and insisting on their right to set the boundaries in the home is an important indication to the child that the family power structure has changed. This may be initially unwelcome and may even induce a temporary escalation in aggression. But both teenagers and children feel safer and more secure in a family where their parents can provide warmth and affection alongside consistent boundaries. Even teenagers who seem very out of control usually respond and moderate their behaviour if parents are able to hold to these guidelines consistently.

Extra considerations for putting in clear boundaries where the child is violent

MODELLING THE BEHAVIOUR YOU WANT TO ENCOURAGE

This is especially important where a child is being violent in the home – children are much more likely to follow what we do than what we say. It's vital not to use violence and put-downs if you expect your children to do the same. It's equally vital that we show our children how to keep firm boundaries if we expect them to learn to do so. This means that, alongside changing how they deal with their children's behaviour, parents will need to have a critical look at their reactions and to identify ways in which they can stop unhelpful patterns of behaviour.

ANALYSING TIMES WHEN THE VIOLENCE AND AGGRESSIVE BEHAVIOUR HAPPENS

It is very useful to go through some specific incidents in detail – this will help you and the parent to make realistic plans for everyone's safety, to spot unhelpful patterns of behaviour and to work out strategies for dealing with the aggression. Try to build a really clear picture of the chain of events, including where people were, who said what to whom, what people did, and what events immediately preceded and followed the aggression. Write down the sequence of events step by step.

Consider, for example, a family who present with a teenage boy, Jacob, who is using violence to his mother following a history of seeing his dad do the same.

Mum has said that she doesn't want Jacob to swear at her, smash things up or hit her.

An analysis of a particular incident might look like this:

1. Mum finds cigarettes in Jacob's bedroom. She removes the cigarettes and hides his playstation in the hall cupboard as a consequence.

2. When Jacob return from school and is watching TV in the living room, mum tells him that she has gone through his room and taken his playstation and he is not getting his allowance this week.

3. Jacob gets angry about her going in his room and swears and shouts that mum's got to give him some money because he owes money to a friend.

4. Mum asks 'Why did you lie about smoking? Why are you always lying? Why should I give my hard-earned money to your useless friends?'

5. Jacob replies by swearing at mum, 'you f*ing bitch' and shouts that she has to pay for the cigarettes as well; he then gets up and goes to his room.

6. Mum follows him and discovers that he has found the playstation and is setting it up.

7. Mum, determined to put in the consequence, tries to get the playstation leads out of Jacob's hands.

8. Jacob refuses to hand the leads over.

9. Mum pulls the leads out of Jacob's hand.

10. As mum tries to take the leads, Jacob grabs her arm and twists it behind her back then pushes her on the bed.

11. Mum walks out crying and they don't talk for the rest of the day. Jacob stays in his room playing on the playstation till the early hours of the morning.

IDENTIFYING UNHELPFUL PATTERNS

Use the above sequence, and the questions below, to think about unhelpful patterns of behaviour and how they can be changed.

Thus in this earlier example, you can emphasise that it was completely wrong of Jacob to hurt and push his mum. But you can also ask, 'How might you handle things differently, so that the consequence gets put in place but you don't put yourself at unnecessary risk?'

You can also ask:

- If you wanted to 'push Jacob's buttons' (i.e. provoke him to perform the behaviour in question) what would you do?* In this situation, mum might identify that, when she asks Jacob 'why are you always lying?', this is an expression of anger and frustration rather than a genuine enquiry about why Jacob does not tell her the truth – and as such is more likely to invite an angry response from Jacob. Mum might also identify that following him to his room wasn't such a good idea (and that it would have been more sensible to remove the playstation leads to somewhere where Jacob could not find them). Also by engaging in a physical struggle with Jacob – trying to take the playstation leads from him – she puts herself at risk.

- Are there typical situations where Jacob gets aggressive?

- Are there times when the same triggers are present, but Jacob manages to stay calm or walk away from trouble?

- What is the payoff for the problem behaviour? What does Jacob get out of hitting or shouting at his mum? What does he avoid?

- How might Jacob have learned to act like this? What poor role modelling is he exposed to (especially from other family members)?

After considering the answers, work together on a plan that could include:

- putting in place rewards and consequences for unwanted behaviour, and holding to these

- mum or dad ending poor role modelling and changing unhelpful patterns

- avoiding the worst examples of parents 'pushing children's buttons'*

- ensuring that abusive behaviour doesn't pay

- increasing praise

- decreasing put-downs

- Jacob avoiding or changing the way he deals with difficult situations.

*BE VERY CAREFUL HERE...

It is important to understand:

- DO NOT let 'avoidance of button pushing' have the consequence that parents stop making reasonable demands of their children.

- DO NOT get into the issue of 'button pushing' between the parents. They need to stop being abusive to each other irrespective of the other's behaviour, and they should take 100 per cent responsibility for their violence or abuse. It is different for children who can't choose to leave the family and who, it might be argued, have less than 100 per cent responsibility for their part in the family dynamic.

- For similar reasons, DO NOT get into a discussion about the ways children push their parents' buttons. Treat behaviours the parents want the children to change as problems by all means – but avoid looking at these as provoking particular parental responses. Parents are 100 per cent responsible for how they deal with their children, whatever behaviours they are dealing with.

Any discussion about button pushing between a child and a parent, or in an adult couple, runs the risk that a victim will be blamed for provoking an abusive response.

Implementing Rewards and Consequences

The following exercise is designed to help parents identify effective consequences for an out-of-control child.

✎ Exercise – Setting consequences for an out-of-control child

1. Look at all the things you do for your children. Consider which could be used as consequences if you stopped doing them. Don't pick anything that will make you feel too guilty, or that you know that your partner will not support.

2. From this list, identify a set of privileges that *you* can completely control (grounding or time-outs require a child's cooperation) and use as consequences. Here are some ideas, and families themselves will come up with many more:

   a. Fines and withholding of financial allowance.

   b. Going on total strike for anywhere between half a day and a week.

   c. Phones – not topping up credit, confiscation of handset or earphones, etc.

   d. Confiscation or locking up of bike.

   e. Transport – not driving children around.

   f. Temporary confiscation of make-up/hair straighteners/hair dryers, etc.

   g. Valued clothes or trainers – temporary confiscation.

   h. Internet or computer – restrictions or removing from the house altogether for a day or two.

    i.   TV – restrictions or removing TV/aerial/cables, etc.

    j.   Favourite foods – not buying or providing.

    k.   For late night stop-outs – an early morning wake-up.

    l.   Silly consequences – parent blows whistle or sings.

    m.   Sharing the information with others influential in the children's life who will then contact them by email or text and simply say they are sorry to hear…

    n.   Calling the police in.

3. Ideally these consequences will be in proportion to the behaviour and will be things the child cares about. However, if the behaviour is frequent, then the consequence will have to be small enough to be applied consistently and realistically. It is better to ground a child for an evening successfully than for a week unsuccessfully, and better to have some small consequence than none at all.

Your first consequence may rely on the child's cooperation but, if you choose a 'cooperative consequence', then you will need a back-up one for the times when the child refuses to take the first consequence (see 'What ifs').

Expect a backlash – 'What ifs'

Clear expectations and being consistent in applying rewards and consequences will be of much greater importance where a child is showing destructive behaviour. In addition, parents will need to plan what to do if consequences don't work or cause an escalation in problem behaviour. Indeed, with a young person who has started to be violent in the home, it's almost certain that the consequences will meet with considerable resistance.

So you'll need to think in advance of all the things that can and will go wrong, and plan for these. As you implement the plan, you are certain to come up against problems – this doesn't mean the plan has gone wrong or doesn't work, it just means you need to develop more 'what ifs'. Tell the parent to expect this, and that the plan will need to be reviewed frequently, especially in the early stages. Unless the parent has been expressly, clearly and repeatedly told 'there *will* be a backlash', then they are likely to take this as evidence that the plan just isn't working, and give up. The worker's role is, as far as possible, to help the family to try and maintain consistency in their reward and consequence systems even where these don't seem to work right away. This may involve permitting the parents to ignore what they can while sticking to rewards and consequences as per the agreement. For example:

Q: What if the child or teenager says 'I don't care' when fined?

A: Ignore – do not respond.

Q: What if children get money from elsewhere (e.g. friends)?

A: Ignore – friends probably won't be able to supply money regularly and a teenager will still want the reward.

Q: What if mum and dad use the fining consequence, but the child or teenager continues to swear more and more and escalates the situation?

A: Exit from the situation to avoid escalation. Deduct money at the end of the evening as usual. Do not keep saying 'That's another fine' as this will wind the child up further.

Q: What if children threaten to throw something, or do throw something, as a result of a consequence?

A: Remind them of the contract, saying 'If you choose NOT to throw that, you will avoid a further consequence.' If they do throw it, they lose more money – stick to the contract.

Some consequences will rely on the cooperation of the person whose behaviour is problematic, so it is important to agree on back-up consequences that are in the control of other family members. For example, if young people have agreed to be grounded for a night because they came in too late the night before, the parents need a back-up consequence in case the young people then refuse to stay in the house. This consequence should be totally in the parents' control – such as a parent refusing to help them out in any way for 24 hours.

SAFETY PLAN

It will also be essential to plan in advance when all else fails and the young person's behaviour becomes risky. Young people often decide to show just how bad they can get when things start to change and parents start to put in place consistent boundaries. Safety must be the number one priority in the end – which means, for example, that a parent might well let a young person who is grounded leave rather than get involved in a physical altercation. Other consequences should follow at a safer future time. For example:

- If a young man simply hits or kicks and then stops or leaves the flat, then the contract is followed – in other words, 'That's a 50p fine'. Mum will not get into an argument, or ask why, or lecture. She will exit from the situation to avoid escalation.

- If the young person starts to smash things or follow mum around spitting, hitting, etc., mum and dad will exit the room for ten minutes so that everybody can calm down.

- If the young person follows them, then they will shut themselves in their bedroom for ten minutes.

- If the young person calms down, mum will speak to him calmly or leave him to have some time-out (whichever he prefers).

- If the young person does not calm down and carries on, then one of the parents should call the police.

IDENTIFYING SUPPORTS

Often a lone parent may feel too disempowered or physically afraid to be able to set boundaries and carry through on consequences for a young person. However, it will help a great deal if the parent gets support from other people for the changes they intend making. It is important to advise parents that this is not a sign of weakness or failure; the saying that 'it takes a village to raise a child' is appropriate here. The supports they choose may include family, friends, neighbours, teachers, parents of the child's friends and even the child's friends themselves. Talk through the possibility of calling the local police if events are really out of hand. It can help to talk with local officers in advance, and consider asking neighbours to call the police if they hear an argument escalating.

Exercise – Utilising wider family and social networks

Ask the parent to list those whom the young person values and holds in some regard. Some of these people may not be useful in this endeavour, either because they would be too abusive (e.g. a previously violent partner) or would not actually disapprove of the unwanted behaviour at all (e.g. some of the young person's peer group).

However, there are likely to be others who have various levels of positive influence on the young person. These could be grandparents, teachers (past or present), aunts and uncles and parents of the young person's friends – they could sometimes even include other peers who might worry for the young person.

Consider how these people could be enlisted to help deter unwanted behaviours. It may be that simply contacting a group of such people to let them know if the young person makes a serious transgression, such as using violence or using drugs recklessly, is an effective consequence. Their just knowing may be sufficient, or you can up the stakes by asking them to express to the young person any concern, disappointment or disapproval they feel. If there is someone else who is able to be more involved still, that person might be enlisted to help set consequences such as removing the TV or refusing to hang out with the young person.

8 Working with Over-authoritarian or Abusive Parenting – Becoming More Child-centred

As we said in the opening chapter, violence towards an intimate partner is often just one part of a pattern of intimidating behaviour, including put-downs, criticism, verbal abuse and emotional cruelty that serve to impose control over others in the home. Abusive fathers also tend to display an overblown sense of entitlement – an expectation that their needs and wishes should come first, that they can opt out of tasks they do not wish to do, and that they should get the last word. This pattern of behaviour often extends to the parenting style of abusive men.

Note: it is not only men who have used violence in the home who display over-controlling parenting styles – parents may behave in this way for a range of reasons. Some of the exercises in this chapter can be used with any parent who wishes to move away from an over-authoritarian parenting style; others are aimed specifically at those who have used violence.

Because a tendency to be over-controlling is part of the problem here, the kinds of behaviour control and discipline strategies we discussed in Chapter 4 are not the first point of intervention in parenting work with abusive fathers. It is more important to focus on *child-centred* parenting with such men. This will involve raising awareness of the effects on children of abusive behaviour (both to the mother and the children themselves) and increasing fathers' understanding of their children's emotional needs and developmental capabilities.

It is also crucial not to ignore that fact that using domestic violence is in itself a significant failure in parenting. Thus any work on parenting needs also to include an awareness that it's just not possible to be a good father and at the same time be abusing, putting down or otherwise undermining the children's mother.

There's an important safety warning to add here. If we look back at the continuum of parenting styles set out in Chapter 1, we can see that, for fathers who have used violence, parenting interventions are most likely to move them from the authoritarian end towards the zone of 'good enough' parenting. However, if violence remains a significant concern, other interventions are likely to be prerequisite to even getting the parent onto this continuum – this book is about working in the aftermath of domestic violence – not in the midst of it. As we said earlier, it will be almost impossible to work on positive parenting with a man who is still using violence and abuse towards the child's mother.

The section on the effects of domestic violence on children (see Chapter 5) is an essential precursor to doing the work in this chapter. Also, if the parent you are working with finds it difficult to move away from resentment towards their partner, or 'the system', refer to the exercise 'The wall' in Chapter 3 as a way of acknowledging and moving beyond such frustrations.

Moving away from over-harsh discipline

This section follows the earlier work to establish a no-smacking commitment and to think about exactly what is meant by child-centred parenting ('Undermining shame and fear-based methods of discipline', see Chapter 4).

✎ Exercise – The parenting log
Aim

- To help a parent who is over-controlling, over-authoritarian and overly 'parent-centred' move towards more child-centred parenting.

When a parent 'disciplines' a child, the parent can usually be seen to have multiple motivations. Even very harsh discipline techniques can be justified in the parent's mind as being for the child's own benefit and teaching an important lesson. Using the parenting continuum (discussed in Chapter 1) allows you to acknowledge both the parent-centred and child-centred motives, and then focus on how parents can achieve only the child-centred objectives using only child-centred methods.

Start this exercise by briefly describing an example situation:

Paul cooks a healthy meal for his son Tom, aged 7. However, Tom says he
doesn't like it and refuses to eat it. Paul at first tells Tom, then shouts at him,

that he should eat the meal. When Tom continues to refuse, Paul shouts louder and sends him to his room for the night.

Then use 'The parenting log' worksheet as a framework for analysing what was going on for Paul in this situation.

ACTIONS

First ask the parent you are working with where Paul's method of discipline, his actions in this situation, might fit on the continuum.

We can see that the sending away and shouting are not going to help Tom internalise long-term values and are instead aimed at getting him quickly out of Paul's space – thus his methods are pretty parent-centred.

MOTIVES

Ask the parent: What did Paul want those actions to achieve? What did he want the child to learn from them? Place each motive on the scale 'from child-centred to parent-centred'.

Paul might have wanted to establish his control and insist on Tom's blind obedience, because he might have felt rejected and angry himself – these would be parent-centred aims. He might also have had child-centred motives – wanting Tom to eat a healthy meal, which would translate into a longer-term aim of wanting Tom to become a healthy discerning eater.

ALTERNATIVES (CHILD-CENTRED NON-ABUSIVE WAYS TO ACHIEVE THE *CHILD-CENTRED* INTENTIONS IDENTIFIED HERE)

Ask the parent what might be non-abusive ways to achieve the child-centred intentions identified. If Paul wants Tom to eat well and make healthy choices, he could perhaps involve Tom more in planning and preparing the meal – taking him shopping, asking him his preferences (perhaps offering limited choices – all healthy). He could cook with Tom, educate him about healthy eating, check Tom is hungry when he cooks his tea – and so on.

EFFECTS (ON TOM, ON PAUL AND ON OTHERS)

In the long term, will Tom be likely to develop a taste for spinach lasagne (or whatever it is his dad has cooked)? And how will he feel about his dad and himself as a result of the incident? What will be the effects if Tom is continually disciplined in this way?

Having gone through an example with parents, you can begin to use the log to think about incidents with their own children when they feel they might not have dealt with discipline situations well.

The parenting log

ACTIONS: Briefly describe your actions and place them on the continuum from child-centred to parent-centred:

Child ├───────────────────────────────────┤ Parent-
-centred   centred

MOTIVES: What did you want those actions to achieve? What did you want your child to learn from them? Place these motives on the continuum from child-centred to parent-centred:

Child ├───────────────────────────────────┤ Parent-
-centred   centred

ALTERNATIVES: Child-centred non-abusive ways to achieve the child-centred intentions identified above.

. . . .

. . . .

. . . .

EFFECTS: What was the impact of your actions?

. . . .

. . . .

. . . .

What would your child learn in the long term if you acted in a child-centred way in this situation?

. . . .

. . . .

. . . .

9 Therapeutic Parenting Following Domestic Violence

Empathetic parenting with children who are 'acting out'

The focus so far has been on helping parents to find consistent, child-centred ways of managing children's behaviour. However, we also need to bear in mind that some of the children we are working with will be showing significant signs of harm from their experience of living with abuse. The more traumatised and less resilient the children are, the more their parents may be faced with the challenge of dealing with their children's sometimes bizarre, sometimes frightening and sometimes terrified 'acting out'. Parents will need a more empathetic and insightful style of parenting to manage this kind of behaviour effectively.

This is of course a lot to ask of parents who may themselves be struggling with the aftermath of difficult experiences. But we can at least offer them some ways of looking at things which help them make some sense of their children's difficulties. (Here we've drawn a lot from the ideas of Dan Hughes (2006) who has written extensively on this topic.)[15]

Children may also be acting out for other reasons – it is worth parents asking themselves what their child's misbehaviour is really about – if it's about other factors such as bullying at school, can they fix that first?

Consistent and loving boundaries

We have looked at how important it is to set consistent boundaries with children. While often experienced as deeply frustrating, boundaries actually make the world more predictable and less scary for children.

However, sometimes children may up the ante and escalate their 'bad' behaviour when parents try to put boundaries in place. Indeed, it can sometimes seem like children are seeking out punishment just so they can blame their parents for how bad they feel. Why might this happen?

Children often feel responsible for trouble in the family, so they can take on a huge sense of shame when frightening and distressing events take place. A sense that there is something very wrong at home can easily lead to children coming to believe that there is something very bad or wrong about them. They may also have a range of other powerful feelings in response to their current or past experience that they simply don't have the language or emotional maturity to express. Children who feel badly about themselves easily misinterpret parental disapproval. Rather than seeing it as disapproval of their behaviour, they take it as confirmation that they themselves are 'bad' or 'wrong'. Acting out may be a way of defending against feeling this way. What this means is that 'standard' parenting techniques may not have the effect that is desired. For instance, time-outs can leave a child who has suffered substantial losses feeling abandoned. Reward schemes and praise depend for their success upon the child feeling worthy enough to deserve praise – some children feel tricked by rewards and praise, or safer with negative attention, because they 'know where they stand'. Similarly, negative consequences may confirm their sense of themselves as bad and undeserving of love.

This doesn't mean that parents should give up providing structure and discipline for their children. However, it does mean that they should:

1. Be careful not to make things worse by reacting to a child's defiance or rejection with out-of-control anger, or by acting in ways that can only increase the child's sense of shame, such as using put-downs or humiliating punishment.

2. Be able to remain calm, empathetic and loving in the face of their child's powerful displays of emotion. Remember that bizarre behaviour usually means that children don't know how to handle what they are feeling and need help. By staying calm, you show your child that the feeling is manageable.

3. Stay emotionally available, acknowledging and offering comfort for the child's hurt feelings, while still providing boundaries for the child.

This last point goes against other theories of behaviour management that would say that, if you comfort children after you tell them off, this 'rewards'

122

them for bad behaviour. However, as we saw in Chapter 5, an important part of the development of secure attachment is in the learning through repeated small breaks in rapport or separations, followed by reconnection and repair. Gradually a build-up of trust occurs, which teaches the child that healing repair and resolution are possible, and models the skills needed for this.

A similar pattern needs to be established with children who are feeling insecure and bad about themselves. Parents need to relate to them in a way that helps them gain or regain that basic trust and awareness that they are loved. There are many minor breaks in the emotional connection between any parent and child when we tell children off or refuse to give them what they want. However, attachment theorists talk of the parental role as being always 'bigger, wiser and kind'.[16] Where breaks in connection or fall-outs are managed with kindness and empathy, then boundary setting becomes a form of containment – helping the child feel safe – *part* of loving rather than opposed to loving.

Repairing breaks in connection

- Note the breaks.

- Understand them.

- Repair them by acknowledging and naming the children's feelings, explaining why the break took place and reassuring them of your love and care for their welfare.

So you might say, 'It's hard when I tell you off, isn't it? I had to stop you doing that because it is dangerous, but I love you and because I love you I care if you get hurt.' In this way the child learns that discipline is to do with the behaviour, not the child and not about the relationship with the parent.

All this also means that we need to think carefully about how we show anger:

- First of all, avoid out-of-control anger – count to ten!

- Bad-mood anger – it's OK to explain to children that you don't have much patience today and why. Let them know it is nothing to do with them. However, do still try to avoid out-of-control anger. Use quick-focused anger instead: 'That's enough! I told you I had less patience today – stop that!'

- Oops – you suddenly yell when you shouldn't have. Repair – 'Sorry, that wasn't your fault. I wish I hadn't done that. I know you've heard too much shouting in your life.' Give comfort and explain.

• Deliberate anger – appropriate and in scale for major violations like hurting people – 'Stop that! That behaviour is outrageous! I am angry because in this house every living thing has to be safe.' Make it quick and loud but don't go on and on. Move into empathy and repair – 'I understand how angry you get. I love you, you're my kid, we're going to work together to find a way to deal with your feelings and keep everyone safe – come have a hug.'

Matching your parenting to your child's emotional age

Distressed children often act like younger children both socially and emotionally. This means that you will need to recognise this and adjust your expectations to match that age so that the children will have experiences of success, not failure. You may need to treat your children as though they were much younger, using more non-verbal methods of soothing and comforting than you might otherwise. For example, a 12-year-old may literally be throwing themselves on the floor and having a '2-year-old tantrum'. If this is the case, you may need to think how you'd deal with a toddler tantrum, and, while also including the extra safety considerations, transfer over those skills (don't get enraged, use distraction or temporary ignoring, keep yourself safe, provide comfort when the storm passes, don't otherwise reward the tantrum).

Understanding and responding to a child who is 'acting out'

It may help to think of children's behaviour as a language by which they show parents their inner world. Rather than thinking 'What has my child done to me?', asking 'What is my child trying to say to me?' will help.

If a child seems to be regressive or acting out, then the parents will benefit from a greater understanding of their child's behaviour. Ask the parents to describe what is going on, then ask them the following:

What might your child be trying to communicate by this behaviour?

What can you or others say to your child?

What can you do?

Use the pointers in the following worksheet to help guide you both in understanding and responding to the child's behaviour.

Understanding and responding to a child who is 'acting out'

- If you try to think about the child's behaviour in relation to what you know it's about, you may be able to take it less personally.

- There is never any point in asking 'Why did you do that?' The child will not know – but you can show curiosity rather than anger:

    I'm interested in why you…

    I'm curious/I wonder why…?

    I wonder if…

- If you have a sense of what your child's behaviour means, it will help if you can name this for the child, for example:

    I can understand why you feel like that…

    I would probably feel like that if I had lived through all that fighting by the age of 6.

    I understand why you find it so hard to accept my love because I've not always been able to be there for you.

    I think you're feeling badly about yourself and it's not surprising because you were so upset by daddy and mummy's fighting.

- Note the current triggers for the behaviour:

    Thank you for showing me how upset you still get at bedtime – I'm sure it scares you because you used to hear so many arguments at night time. There won't be any fighting tonight.

- Work with the trigger situations differently – for example, you might change the bedtime routine to make your child feel safer. You may find yourself having to treat a 10-year-old more like a toddler in this respect.

- Make environmental changes to make it harder for the children to get in trouble, so, if they are stealing money, don't leave your purse lying around.

- Set realistic – not punitive – consequences.

- Don't allow the child to control the emotional environment of the home. When children act out, it tends to invite raging or terrified responses in their parents. As far as possible parents should try to avoid these responses by remaining empathetic.

- Try to maintain a loving attitude, and keep playfulness and good times in your routine with your child.

(Adapted from Family Futures, www.familyfutures.co.uk)

10 Parental Separation

Being child-centred with the other parent

As we said earlier, it is just not possible to be a good parent and at the same time be abusing, putting down or otherwise undermining the children's other parent. In relation to domestic violence, an assault on a child's mother is an assault on the child's world, and the effects of this can be more serious, especially in young children, than assaults on children themselves.

The need to treat the other parent with respect for the sake of the children applies whether or not the parents live together – research shows that, while most children do not suffer long term from the disruption caused by parental separation, they are much more likely to do so if there is continuing conflict between the parents.

The following exercise extends the idea of child-centred parenting to how parents might behave when they are in dispute with each other. The key message is that, to parent in a child-centred way, you will often have to set aside your own anger, sense of injustice or desire to win in disputes with your partner. The question to keep returning to is, no matter how difficult or unfair it might feel, how do you behave if you hold the best interests of your children in mind?

✎ **Exercise – In whose best interests?**
Aims

- To help parents begin to separate their anger and their interests from the children's interests.

- To increase parents' understanding and empathy for the range of ways they may use their children in arguments with their partners.

- To help parents find alternatives to such behaviours.

The following role play involves a man called John, his partner May, and their child Jasmine (aged 8).

If working with mothers, you will be focusing on the options for May. If working with fathers, focus on John's options. Establish with your client that you are going to look at two ways that the parent in question can act in the following scenarios:

1. In a child-centred way – where the parent's actions are solely driven by what is in the best interests of the child.

2. In a way that is driven by the parent's anger towards the other parent and putting personal wishes and feelings first.

Tell the parent that you are going to describe a scenario and that you will then imagine together how it might go on:

SCENARIO 1

John and May are in the middle of an argument about the state of the house and who does more cleaning. John and May are both shouting at each other and both are sure that they do far more of the housework than the other.

Ask your clients to put themselves into May's or John's shoes and to say how that parent might act if solely driven by anger and is putting personal wishes and feelings first. Get a brief continuation of the story.

Example: John ignores May and carries on shouting at her. When May won't back down, he may escalate the argument and start to push her around.

Then ask your client to imagine being in Jasmine's shoes. Ask:

What would it be like to see her mum and dad shouting at each other?

Would it be different in any way if Jasmine was aware that John had hit May in the past?

What might Jasmine tell herself about what is going on?

What options does Jasmine have in that situation?

What might Jasmine do?

Ask your clients to put themselves into John's or May's shoes again, but this time to say how that parent might act if only holding Jasmine's best interests in mind.

You can then go on to use different scenarios, to explore how the parent might act when being parent-centred, or child-centred. Start with some of the scenarios offered here.

Once your clients have the hang of this, you can go on to think through some examples drawn from their own experience.

Note: It may be useful to set out two extra chairs and get clients to move to a different chair when thinking about things from the parent's and from the child's point of view, then to return to their own chair when reflecting on what the exercise brings up for them.

SCENARIO 2

John shouts at Jasmine. May says he's too strict and should let her do whatever she was doing.

SCENARIO 3 – FOR FATHERS

John and May are now separated – John takes Jasmine out for the day. Jasmine complains about May, says she doesn't help her enough with her homework and mentions that she has a new boyfriend. Jasmine says she misses daddy.

SCENARIO 3 – FOR MOTHERS

John and May are now separated – John takes Jasmine out for the day. When she gets back, Jasmine complains to May that John has not given her enough attention because he has a new girlfriend now. She also says he made mean comments about May being tight with money.

SCENARIO 4 – FOR FATHERS

John goes to collect Jasmine for a visit but May has forgotten and says that he can't have her today – she is going to meet a friend.

SCENARIO 4 – FOR MOTHERS

John is meant to have Jasmine every other weekend and also Thursday nights. He has been half an hour late for the last two handovers and missed the one before altogether. On this particular day he finally arrives an hour and a half late, causing May to be extremely late for her friend's birthday lunch.

SCENARIO 5

John is handing Jasmine back to her mother and they begin to discuss Jasmine's birthday next Thursday. Both John and May are wanting her that day.

SCENARIO 6

May asks for money for Jasmine's new shoes. Jasmine is present. John feels that he has given enough this month.

Some advice for parents who've separated following domestic violence

When working with victims of domestic violence, it is tempting to think that, if the victim could just separate from the abusive partner, things would be OK. Unfortunately, the truth of the matter is that the period during and after separation is a time of considerably increased risk. The end of any relationship may give rise to powerful feelings of anger, resentment and fear of loss. However, some abusive men will react violently to feelings of powerlessness and hurt, and dangerously escalate their attempts to maintain control over their ex. This is why the most severe attacks often happen around the time of separation (this is the time of greatest risk for domestic violence homicides) and even after separation women often go through a sustained period of harassment or stalking. Of the thousands of incidents of domestic violence against women recorded each year in the UK, more than a third happen when the couple are no longer living together.

After separation, abusive partners usually remain involved in their ex-partners' lives in one way or another, often through contact with their children. Unfortunately, the abusive and controlling tactics used within the relationship often extend to the management of contact arrangements. It is very common for child contact to be used as a pretext to keep tabs on an ex-partner, to continue the conflict and to undermine the mother's attempts to establish a new life and new relationships. It is also our experience that some men seeking contact after a violent relationship has ended seem more preoccupied with securing their 'rights' to contact than with thinking about their children's welfare.

We have included here a set of 'tips' for parents who are separating after domestic violence. The key message to give to parents is that separation in itself is not harmful to children – at least one in three children under 16 in the UK will experience parental separation. The research on parental separation indicates that the great majority of children are functioning well within two years of separation. However, this is not true in all cases – around 20–25 per cent of children from separated parents experience serious social or emotional problems (compared to less than 10% of young people from intact families).

Unsurprisingly, the evidence shows that family conflict both before and after separation is a big determinant of whether the child will be one of the 75 per cent who fare OK or the 25 per cent who don't.

The parents we work with, in particular the abusive parent, may be caught up in powerful feelings of anger or even outright hatred towards each other and hold a deep suspicion of each other's motives. In such circumstances, it is a huge challenge to maintain even a neutral stance towards the other parent for the benefit of the child. Nevertheless, the basic message, that *the hurt children feel about separation can be healed, but continuing conflict will continue the hurt,* is crucial for parents to hold on to in their dealings with each other and their children.

Tips for fathers

If you are a father who has been abusive in a relationship with the mother of your children and you are now separated, it can be very difficult knowing how best to deal with the children and your ex-partner. The following guidelines may need to be adapted because every situation is different.

- It just doesn't matter what the circumstances were, or whose fault you think it was, or if you think you have changed, or if it wasn't in front of the children or if you think they didn't get your side of the story: children just don't like people hurting either of their parents.

- Your hurting or abusing their mum almost certainly affected them and probably still does. They may be scared, upset or angry at you.

- Understand that your children are likely to be very confused about their feelings for both you and their mum. It is possible to feel lots of different emotions at the same time and children's feelings can also change quite quickly over time. Pre-teen children are usually concrete thinkers who prefer to see the world as black and white – good guys and bad guys – rather than in shades of grey. Thus loving a father who has been violent can be bewildering for them.

Boundaries

- Minimise situations where your children see you and your ex-partner together. If there is a high level of conflict or continuing threats, no contact at all between parents is the best thing for children.

- Don't think you have to be friends with your ex-partner. 'Co-operative colleagues' is the ideal, not 'perfect pals' – in other words, aim for a working relationship rather than friendship. Letting go of a partner when you may not be fully ready, or under circumstances which feel unfair, is one of the hardest things in the world to do. If you try to avoid all unnecessary contact, the resentment and grief stages will pass more easily for both of you.

- Be clear about your boundaries with your ex. Even casual or trivial displays of affection between ex-partners can be confusing for children, delaying their coming to terms with the separation.

- 'Not in front of the children' applies even more now to arguments. Be insistent that you don't argue or have serious discussions when the children are around. This is not the time to discuss arrangements or issues (do this by phone or email). Once there has been conflict in a family, raised voices can have a different meaning for children for years to come. You can't win in this situation because many children are hypersensitive to tone of voice, body language and facial expressions, and any negativity between you will be stressful to them.

- Don't let your kids see you being abusive to anyone. That even includes other drivers on the roads. You may scare them and will make it harder for them to rebuild their trust in you.

- Stop shouting at your children, threatening them, putting them down or hitting them. But continue to discipline them by rewarding good behaviour and by explaining why bad behaviour is wrong and by setting consequences. They may act like you've gone soft at first but they will gradually learn to respect your new way of doing things. Children who have been through parental separation and conflict need gentle treatment for a prolonged period to help them through.

- Avoid criticism of the other parent as far as possible. Not only is this upsetting and stressful for children but criticism can backfire because children often defend, openly or mentally, a parent who is attacked. If the children tell you that your ex-partner is criticising you, don't believe you can even the score by criticising her. Just state that this is just their mother's opinion and you don't agree – people often see the same situation differently. Try not to show your anger. It may be helpful to find someone neutral, such as a counsellor, for the children to talk to about this. Don't expect the children to be able to stand up to their mother – even if they know she is exaggerating or they say they hate her criticising you, they probably won't be able to say anything to her.

- Avoid talking to other people about your ex-partner when the kids are around because, even if you can resist being critical, your friends and family will often say things that are hurtful to the children.

Accountability

- Try to model being accountable for your behaviour irrespective of whether you think their mother is doing so too. Think of this as a way of teaching your children how to face up to their own mistakes rather than as anything to do with arguing for their loyalties (although they are very likely to appreciate your frank honesty). Don't criticise their mum but do own up to your own faults.

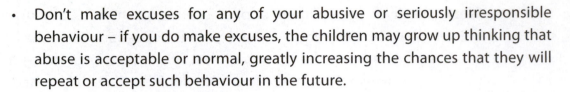

- Don't make excuses for any of your abusive or seriously irresponsible behaviour – if you do make excuses, the children may grow up thinking that abuse is acceptable or normal, greatly increasing the chances that they will repeat or accept such behaviour in the future.

- You might say something like this but in your own words: 'I have done some things that are not right such as hitting mummy or scaring you. I am really sorry for doing these things and for how much it has upset you. A lot of families have problems like this even though they might not tell people about it. I still love you. It isn't even a bit your fault – you're too young/small to be able to control us or to stop us arguing. There is no excuse for me hitting mummy or you. Violence is wrong, no matter how angry you get. No matter what you do, you don't deserve to be hit.'

Loyalty

- Children often struggle very hard to be loyal to their parents. Loyalty conflicts can be intense (usually worst around ages 12–14) with children sometimes not only turning against new partners but against brothers and sisters and even against their mother (often temporarily) as they try to resolve their loyalty conflicts. Some children say they feel as if they are pawns in their parents' games or that they are being torn in two. It can be an extremely hard balancing act – trying to protect your children without taking part in a tug-of-war.

- Loyalty conflicts may make it very hard for your children to open up to you about their mother or about their feelings. Don't push them to tell you everything. Don't interrogate them about what happens with their mother or they will learn to lie or clam up. They may also find it hard to talk to you about the situation because they are protective of you and don't want to see you upset.

- Don't assume that your ex has 'poisoned the children against you'. They are most likely angry with you for their own reasons. They may also be angry with you because their mum is upset and they feel loyal to her. That doesn't mean she's done this on purpose. Children usually sus right away when one parent is trying to turn them against the other and, more often than not, they end up very angry with the manipulative parent.

Mum's new partner

- Don't jump to conclusions about the mother's new partner. Often the new person around can be intensely hated because of the loyalty issues described earlier, or can represent the new, fun person around who's really working to win them over – in short, your children could really like or hate the new man around their mother without it showing much about what he's actually like. They may tell you they like him just to get at you if they feel confused or angry with you. Or they may say they hate him just to please you.

- Don't think for a minute that, because their mother finds a new partner, he will replace you. Even if the children really like him (for which you should be glad, even if it pains you), the bond they have with him will be nothing like that which they have with you. Sometimes new people can be a lot of fun, without really mattering.

Contact

- You want to see your child. It's natural and normal for you to feel that way. For your child and your ex, it might not be so straightforward. You're the adult and the parent, so, no matter what's happened, no matter what the reasons are for the lack of contact, no matter who or what you think is to blame for this, you have to be able to put all this aside and do what's best for your child.

- The good news is that most women, even after violence, DO want their children to know their dad and for the dad to be involved regularly, provided it is SAFE for all of them, including her. You might have to do some work to convince everyone that it is safe and they might take a long time to believe you. You will just have to be patient. Just because you think you have changed, you can't expect everyone else to feel the same way.

- Beware of making unrealistic demands at first and instead let trust build. If you use contact reliably and not ever in bargaining other things (e.g. finances) or being abusive, then your ex is more likely to come to recognise the benefits of it to herself and the children.

- No matter how long it takes before your child is ready for contact, you will still have to make sure that this is OK for their mum. If she is still frightened of you, it will be vital to make sure that the contact doesn't make this worse; otherwise this will also affect your children. For example, you may have to arrange to pick the children up from a child contact centre, or start off by having only indirect contact for a while, or be supervised at a child contact centre or through an online service such as Dadspace.[17]

- Don't over-commit – regularity is more important for children than frequency. It is far better that children see their father predictably once a month than fortnightly but with lots of cancellations. If every day is a potential contact day, then every day can be a disappointment or rejection to them.

- Be very reliable with whatever contact you have. If you aren't, it confuses children and creates opportunities for more trauma and stress. At times of great upset and change, creating new reliable routines is vital.

- Think of yourself as having responsibilities to your children rather than rights to them. Ask yourself how well you are fulfilling your responsibilities in the circumstances, rather than whether you're getting what you want from this.

- Make the most of the contact you have – write letters, take pictures and make albums of your time together, talk a lot to your children about their lives and interests as well as your own and your family's. Do activities that allow for interaction – from playing, to helping with homework or cooking together to special memorable trips out (although these should not dominate your time with the children).

- You can't make it up to your children by spoiling them – they will see through it and lose respect for you if you try.

Finally

- Dealing with all this is like walking through an emotional minefield! Don't feel that you are a failure if you need to ask for help for yourself or for your children. A few children may need a lot of help but some benefit from just a few counselling sessions with an independent adult, or time with a loving grandparent.

- Looking after yourself is very important for your children's well-being. Getting your own life back on track may be the best way to help them.

- If the other parent is being irresponsible, you have to be more responsible with regard to the kids. Don't ever let your adherence to any of these guidelines depend on how well the children's mother is doing. Don't sink to her level or play tit-for-tat with your children's well-being.

(Adapted from Lundy Bancroft (2003) *Why Does He Do That?* Berkeley Publishing Group.)

Tips for mothers

If you are a mother who has left an abusive relationship, it can be very difficult knowing how best to deal with the children and your ex-partner. The following guidelines may need to be adapted because every situation is different.

- Be very clear that exposing children to ongoing violence and abuse of their mothers is also emotional abuse of them. Even if you were struggling to prioritise your own safety, you don't have the right to impose this on your children. Don't make light of your ex-partner's abusing you in any way (swearing at you, shouting, putting you down, any form of threats or intimidation).

Boundaries

- Minimise situations where children see you and your ex-partner together. With high conflict or continuing threats, no contact at all between parents is the best thing for children.

- Don't think you have to be friends with your ex-partner. 'Co-operative colleagues' is the ideal, not 'perfect pals' – in other words, aim for a working relationship rather than friendship. Abusive men are often possessive and may try to remain emotionally involved with their ex-partner (or have power over them), which means that signs of friendship may be misinterpreted or used against you.

- Be very clear about boundaries. Don't let him invade your space or your time. Not only can this be dangerous or upsetting for you, it also confuses children and creates opportunities for more trauma and stress. Even casual or trivial displays of affection between ex-partners can be confusing for children, delaying their coming to terms with the separation.

- 'Not in front of the children' applies even more to arguments. Be insistent that you don't argue or have serious discussions when the children are around. This is not the time to discuss arrangements or issues (do this by phone or email). Once there has been violence in a family, raised voices can have a different meaning for children for years to come. You can't win in this situation because many children are hypersensitive to tone of voice, body language and facial expressions, and any negativity between you will be stressful to them.

- If the other parent is being irresponsible, you have to be more responsible with regard to the kids. Don't sink to his level!

- Although you may be forced to take more responsibility because he is taking less, don't take on all his responsibility or think that you can make him be a good father. Encouraging contact is good (ONLY if safe, of course) but taking over all the responsibility often means setting your kids up for disappointment in the future.

Permitting contact

- Beware of unrealistic commitments. He may want (or demand) extremely regular contact at first. Some irresponsible fathers disappear for a time then want intensive contact as if to make up for their absence. He may mean well or he may simply be trying to maintain his involvement with you, but either way, if he is not going to continue this indefinitely, it can lead to further disappointments for your children. If he starts off phoning daily, for example, (which may be checking up on you) they will be disappointed when this inevitably becomes less frequent. Regularity is usually more important than frequency. It is far better that children see their father predictably once a month than fortnightly but with lots of cancellations. If every day is a potential contact day, then every day can be a disappointment or rejection to them. Their anger at this is quite likely to be directed at you.

- Avoid criticism of the other parent as far as possible. Not only is this upsetting and stressful for children but criticism can backfire because children often defend, openly or mentally, a parent who is attacked. If the children tell you that your ex-partner is criticising you, don't believe you can even the score by criticising him. If he is lying, then tell the children the truth (but never all the gory or adult details). If it is a matter of opinion, then just state that this is just their father's opinion and you don't agree. It may be helpful to find someone neutral, such as a counsellor, for the children to talk to about this. Don't expect the children to be able to stand up to their father – even if they know he is lying or they say they hate him criticising you, they probably won't be able to say anything to him.

- Avoid talking to other people about your ex-partner when the kids are around because, even if you can resist being critical, your friends and family will often say things that are hurtful to the children.

- Avoiding criticism does not mean you should lie to the children to minimise their father's faults or to protect their feelings. Making excuses for abusive or seriously irresponsible behaviour means that they may grow up thinking that abuse is acceptable or normal, greatly increasing the chances that they will repeat such behaviour in the future. Saying things like 'You know your father loves you' if he hasn't made contact for six months is confusing as well as being untrue (if he does love them, they don't know it). Saying, 'He only acts like that because he's an alcoholic' may contain some truth but is also suggesting that he does not have responsibility for his abusive behaviour. Don't excuse abuse! It is important to state that abuse is wrong, but try to condemn the behaviour not the person.

- Understand that your children are likely to be very confused about their feelings for their father. It is possible to feel lots of different emotions at the same time and children's feelings can also change quite quickly over time. Pre-teen children are usually concrete thinkers who prefer to see the world as black and white – good guys and bad guys – rather than in shades of grey. Thus loving a father who has been violent can be bewildering for them.

Loyalty

- Children often struggle very hard to be loyal to an irresponsible or rejecting parent. Loyalty conflicts can be intense (usually worst around ages 12–14) with children sometimes not only turning against new partners but against brothers and sisters and even against their mothers (often temporarily) as they try to resolve their loyalty conflicts. Some children say they feel as if they are pawns in their parents' games or that they are being torn in two. It can be an extremely hard balancing act trying to protect your children without taking part in a tug-of-war.

- Children struggling to be loyal to their father are actually more likely to reject a step-father than are children who have a happy, stable relationship with their own father. Never, ever, suggest that a step-father is a substitute for their natural father and don't bother to point out that he is better because this is just as likely to strengthen their loyalty to their father.

- Don't think that you have to get a partner for the sake of your children. This is not necessary, not likely to help them, and is a very bad reason to re-partner.

- Loyalty conflicts may make it very hard for them to open up to you about their father or about their feelings. Don't push them to tell you everything. Don't interrogate them about what happens with their father or they will learn to lie or clam up. They may also find it hard to talk to you about the situation because they are protective of you and don't want to see you upset.

- Don't add extra stress to your children's lives if it can be avoided, especially in the year or two after a separation. Avoid unnecessary moves, changes of school, on-again/off-again relationships (with their father or others).

- Looking after yourself is very important for your children's well-being. Getting your own life back on track may be the best way to help them. Children often don't have any respect for a parent who lives to serve them. It is definitely possible to be too child-focused. Get a life!

- Try not to feel guilty about what the children have gone through in the past – you didn't plan it and you've done your best to stop it. Many women say they feel guilty about having exposed the children to abuse (by choosing the wrong partner) and also feel guilty for leaving him. Clearly this is illogical, so why not stop feeling guilty for both?

- You can't make it up to your children by being soft – they need clear boundaries and firm consequences. If you are too soft, they often won't respect you. You need to deal with their behaviour regardless of where it is coming from. If there were too many rules or harsh punishments when you were with their father, it may be tempting to now have too few rules and no consequences. Don't fall into this trap! Punishment does not need to be physical punishment. Children who have been abused or who have witnessed abuse don't need more violence, so find alternatives to hitting them.

- Don't accept abuse from anyone – including your kids. If you do, it is likely to get worse as the abuser loses more respect for you over time. If your children have seen you abused by more than one person (including another child), it will be harder to regain their respect. Avoid, if at all possible, exposing them to your being put down or abused in any way by anyone. It is important that all abuse is taken seriously. If they see an older brother or sister abusing you and there are no consequences, they are more likely to copy this behaviour. It can thus be important to have consequences even if these appear (in the short term) to have no effect whatsoever on the abusive child.

- Beware of saying that a child is like his father. You may hope to change his behaviour or attitudes because he doesn't want to be like his father but not only may he have mixed feelings about being like his father but such a belief can be a self-fulfilling prophecy and he may believe he is doomed to repeat his father's behaviours.

- If your ex-partner is not likely to stay around for the long haul, consider if his family can play an ongoing role in your children's lives. Sometimes regular (which doesn't have to mean frequent) access with grandparents can be a safe way of keeping some contact with their father without giving him so many opportunities to disappoint them and without giving him power over you. Even if he has no contact with his family, maintaining these links helps some children.

Dealing with all this is like walking through an emotional minefield! Don't feel that you are a failure if you need to ask for help for yourself or for your children. A few children may need a lot of help but some benefit from just a few counselling sessions with an independent adult. Beware of counsellors with preconceived ideas: especially if they blame the victim or seem to believe that you or your kids are inevitably damaged for life!

(Adapted from Lundy Bancroft (2003) *Why Does He Do That?* Berkeley Publishing Group)

Bibliography

This book is based on training sessions we have run with hundreds of professionals over the past ten years. In these trainings and in our direct work with parents we have drawn on the best practice we could find in the field and so are hugely indebted to the work of others. We have put a selective bibliography below.

Bancroft, L. and Silverman, J. (2002) *The Batterer as Parent: Addressing the Impact of Domestic Violence on Family Dynamics.* Thousand Oaks, CA: Sage Publications.

Gerhardt, S. (2004) *Why Love Matters: How Affection Shapes a Baby's Brain.* Abingdon: Routledge.

Hughes, D. (2006) *Building the Bonds of Attachment.* Lanham, MD: Jason Aronson Publishers.

Humphreys, C., Thiara, R.K., Mullender, A. and Skamballis. A. (2006) *Talking to My Mum: A Picture Workbook for Workers, Mothers and Children Affected by Domestic Abuse.* London: Jessica Kingsley Publishers.

Morgan, A. (2000) *What Is Narrative Therapy? An Easy-To-Read Introduction.* Adelaide: Dulwich Centre Publications.

Scott, K., Francis, K., Crooks, C. and Kelly, T. (2005) *Caring Dads: Helping Fathers Value their Children.* Bloomington, IN: Trafford Publishing.

Seigel, D. and Hartzell, M. (2003) *Parenting From The Inside Out.* New York: Tarcher/ Penguin.

Sells, S. (2001) *Parenting Your Out-of-Control Teenager.* New York: St Martin's Press.

White, M. (2007) *Maps of Narrative Practice.* New York: W.W. Norton.

Notes

1. See, for instance, Catherine Humphreys and Audrey Mullender (n.d.) 'Children and domestic violence: A research overview of the impact on children.' A Research in Practice pamphlet. Available at www.icyrnet.net/UserFiles/mullender. pdf, accessed on 22 November 2010.

2. Sturge, C. and Glaser, D. (2000) 'Contact and domestic violence: The experts' court report.' *Family Law 30*, 615–629.

3. Stanley, N., Miller, P., Richardson Foster, H. and Thomson, G. (2010) *Children and Families Experiencing Domestic Violence: Police and Children's Social Services Responses*, January. NSPCC (www.nspcc.org.uk/inform).

4. For a review, see Humphreys, C. (2006) ECM Briefing on Domestic violence and Child Abuse, Research in Practice, Making Research Count, for the Department for Education and Skills. Available at www.rip.org.uk/publications/ecm-research-briefings

5. See, for example, Webster-Stratton, C. (2006) *The Incredible Years*. Seattle, WA: The Incredible Years. See also Steele, M., Marigna, M., Tallo, J. and Johnson, R. (2000) *Strengthening Families, Strengthening Communities: An Inclusive Parenting Programme*. Race Equality Unit.

6. Epston, D. (2009) 'New genre of a narrative therapy approach to the problems of young people and their families/communities: Workshop notes 2009'. Available at www.narrativeapproaches.com/narrative%20papers%20folder/ DEpstonworkshop09.htm, accessed on 22 November 2010.

7. The metaphor of 'The wall' is taken from the 'Caring Dads' programme – see Scott, K., Francis, K., Crooks, C. and Kelly, T. (2005) *Caring Dads: Helping Fathers Value their Children*. Bloomington, IN: Trafford Publishing.

8. The idea of the child/parent-centred parenting continuum comes from the 'Caring Dads' programme (see www.caringdadsprogram.com, accessed on 22 November 2010).

9. Iwi, K. and Todd, J. (2000) *Working Towards Safety: A Guide to Domestic Violence Intervention Work*. London: DVIP.

10. Seigel, D. and Hartzell, M. (2003) *Parenting From The Inside Out*. New York: Tarcher/Penguin.

11. See the review by Arlna Ulman and Murray A. Straus (2000) 'Violence by children against mothers in relation to violence between parents and corporal punishment by parents.' *Journal of Comparative Family Studies 34*, 41–60.

12. See two linked articles by Eddie Gallagher (2004) 'Parents victimised by their children' and 'Youth who victimise their parents.' *Australian and New Zealand Journal of Family Therapy 25*, 1, 1–12 and *25*, 2, 94–105. These articles, and other extensive resources, are available at www.anzjft.com/pages/sample_articles.php, accessed on 25 November 2010.

13. White, M. (2009) *Maps of Narrative Practice.* New York: Tarcher/Penguin.

14. Morgan, A. (2000) *What is Narrative Therapy? An Easy-to-Read Introduction.* Adelaide: Dulwich Centre Publications.

15. Hughes, D. (2006) *Building the Bonds of Attachment.* Lanham, MD: Jason Aronson Publishers.

16. Bowlby, J. (1988) *A Secure Base: Parent–Child Attachment and Healthy Human Development.* New York: Basic Books. Also, Marvin, R., Cooper, G., Hoffman, K. and Powell, B. (2002) 'The Circle of Security project: attachment-based intervention with caregiver–pre-school child dyads.' *Attachment & Human Development 4*, 1, 107–124.

17. See www.respect.uk.net, retrieved 22 November 2010.